SCIENTIFIC AMERICAN EXPLORES BIG IDEAS

Food Systems of the Future

The Editors of *Scientific American*

SCIENTIFIC AMERICAN EDUCATIONAL PUBLISHING

New York

Published in 2024 by Scientific American Educational Publishing
in association with **The Rosen Publishing Group**
2544 Clinton Street, Buffalo NY 14224

Contains material from Scientific American®, a division of Springer Nature America, Inc., reprinted by permission, as well as original material from The Rosen Publishing Group®.

First Edition

Scientific American
Lisa Pallatroni: Project Editor

Rosen Publishing
Jennifer Lombardo: Compiling Editor
Michael Moy: Senior Graphic Designer

Cataloging-in-Publication Data
Names: Scientific American Educational Publishing, editor.
Title: Food systems of the future / the editors of Scientific American.
Description: New York : Scientific American Educational Publishing, 2024. | Series: Scientific American explores big ideas | Includes bibliographical references and index. | Audience: Grades 10-12
Identifiers: LCCN 2023034882 | ISBN 9781725350373 (library binding) | ISBN 9781725350366 (paperback) | ISBN 9781725350380 (ebook)
Subjects: LCSH: Food supply–Environmental aspects–Juvenile literature. | Sustainable agriculture–Juvenile literature. | Food security–Juvenile literature.
Classification: LCC HD9000.5 .F59959 2024 | DDC 338.1/9–dc23/eng/20230809
LC record available at https://lccn.loc.gov/2023034882

Manufactured in the United States of America
Websites listed were live at the time of publication.

Cover: gan chaonan/Shutterstock.com

CPSIA Compliance Information: Batch # CWSA24.
For Further Information contact Rosen Publishing at 1-800-237-9932.

CONTENTS

INTRODUCTION

In an era of rapidly evolving global challenges, few issues are as critical and far-reaching as the future of our food systems. As the world's population continues to grow, urbanize, and demand higher quality nutrition, our traditional approaches to food production, distribution, and consumption are being put to the test. Climate change, resource scarcity, social inequality, and health crises have all converged to create a pressing need for innovative and sustainable solutions that can nourish a growing world sustainably and equitably.

Food Systems of the Future explores various aspects of the interconnected web of processes and actors that shape how food is produced, processed, transported, marketed, and consumed. The articles included here unravel the complexities of our current food systems, examining their strengths and weaknesses, and exploring the untapped opportunities for improvement. They challenge long-standing assumptions and shed light on the innovative initiatives already underway that offer glimpses of what lies ahead. Through the lens of sustainability, resilience, and inclusivity, these authors uncover the strategies, technologies, and policies that have the potential to revolutionize how we feed ourselves and future generations. They analyze the dynamic interplay between agriculture, nutrition, environment, culture, and economics, recognizing that no single solution exists in isolation but instead requires holistic and integrated thinking.

While acknowledging the enormity of the challenges the world faces, this volume is ultimately a celebration of human ingenuity, creativity, and resilience. It is a call to action for individuals, communities, and institutions to reimagine and redesign our food systems, guided by principles of sustainability, social justice, and well-being. By embracing cutting-edge technologies, regenerative practices, and inclusive governance, we can create a future where food is not only a source of nourishment but also a catalyst for positive change.

Section 1: Problems Facing Food Systems

Our Food Systems Are in Crisis

By Izabella Koziell

While global leaders gathered in New York City last month to discuss the climate crisis, it is possible that we are missing the bigger picture. It is not only a climate crisis that we have on our hands; it is a full-blown planetary emergency, and agriculture is both a source and a potential solution.

In the last year alone, African swine fever has left over five million pigs dead, fires have blazed across the Amazon to clear land for farming, devastating landslides have been triggered by intensive vegetable farming in the mountainous areas of India, and dead zones in waterways have continued to expand due in part to agricultural runoffs. Let us not forget the dangerous declines in biodiversity driven largely by agriculture, as reported in a landmark intergovernmental report this year.

These are happening in addition to and not just as a cause of climate change and yet will most certainly make the impacts of climate change far worse.

So, the decisions made in the next few decades will have huge ramifications for the future of our planet, and getting our food systems right is at the heart of this. Current practices are contributing to the problem, all in an effort to produce the record amounts of food needed to feed our global population.

But can agriculture accomplish this, admittedly massive, task while reducing its negative impacts at the same time?

The Green Revolution enabled food production to outpace population increases, but it was this very progress that contributed to large-scale land and water degradation, biodiversity losses and increased greenhouse gas emissions.

Now, the productivity of 23 per cent of global land has declined, and about 75 percent of freshwater is used just for agriculture.

Even if the climate crisis was miraculously solved tomorrow, agricultural production would still be racing down the road to unsustainability–failing to deliver diverse diets for all, income equality or the health and well-being of the world's forests, soils and water.

Currently, so-called solutions are often heralded as the solution to climate change–from planting millions of trees or sequestering carbon in farms. But placing all bets on any one of these alone will not resolve the myriad challenges facing the agriculture sector and those whose livelihoods depend on it.

So, what will?

We need a radical transformation of food production, and we already know a lot about how to make this happen.

The first step is to face the reality that agriculture must be intertwined with preserving and restoring natural resources such as water, land, ecosystems and biodiversity of plants and animals, a practice known as sustainable natural resource management (NRM).

NRM demands better understanding and examining of how agricultural practices affect these resources wherever possible, whether positively or negatively. For instance, what effects do new irrigation systems (which benefit farmers) have on wetland systems, biodiversity and the availability of drinking water for nearby cities?

The second step is to actively manage the various trade-offs and synergies that exist between agricultural growth and the environment. Policies that promote diverse diets, for instance, can enrich soils and build biodiversity through the introduction of alternative crops or forgotten foods, but they may mean convincing people accustomed to other foods to eat them. Knorr, for instance, is collaborating with Sodexo and World Wildlife Fund–U.K. to introduce ancient ingredients into products as a way of enhancing diversity.

Other agricultural innovations, such as solar irrigation technology, are helping to build positive environmental outcomes while countering potential risks. Yes, it is a climate solution: replacing carbon-inefficient diesel pumps. But it also helps farmers access ever-scarcer water resources and endure periods of extreme drought. While "free" solar electricity may lead to overpumping of groundwater, new models incentivize farmers to sell excess electricity to the grid instead.

Thirdly, encouraging and investing in future solutions that tackle these multiple complexities at once will help deliver more food in ways that nourish both people and the environment. This is not a zero-sum game.

But we also know that overcoming barriers to political and institutional apathy, vested interests, up-front costs of innovations and insufficient investment in the right type research and development is a critical aspect of this effort also—and that change in these areas is difficult and slow.

That is why we are establishing a Commission on Sustainable Agriculture Intensification, which will look at the key barriers to change by bringing together eminent scientists, policy-makers, business leaders, farmer organizations and others to gather and critically assess the best solutions, technologies and—most importantly—incentives that will drive change.

Results from this two-year-long process will provide the evidence, recommendations and engagement needed to build a roadmap that can bring about this transformation. It is no wonder, then, that the recent Global Commission on Adaptation report calls to double funding for agricultural research through the global research partnership CGIAR.

Solutions such as these will help the world, particularly those in the most vulnerable areas of the global South. to deliver more food sustainably, while building environmental health and climate resilience.

After all, it is our natural resource base that will keep humanity alive and thriving in the long term. Our food systems need to reflect this. Let us not just fulfil short-term needs that place our long-term food security at stake.

The views expressed are those of the author(s) and are not necessarily those of Scientific American.

About the Author

Izabella Koziell is a program director at WLE, a research institute focused on the conservation and preservation of Earth's water, land and ecosystems.

The Effects of COVID-19 Will Ripple through Food Systems

By Laura Poppick

As winter gives way to spring, farmers across the U.S. are ramping up for the growing season—hiring workers, purchasing materials and taking orders. But measures to rein in the COVID-19 pandemic may derail some of those efforts, experts say. "Everybody is scrambling to figure out what to do," says Gail Feenstra, deputy director of the Sustainable Agriculture Research and Education Program at the University of California, Davis, who studies food systems and supply chains. "There's just a lot of disruption."

Though the extent of the blow to U.S. food production is unclear—and will depend on how long the pandemic and countermeasures last—widespread food shortages are unlikely anytime soon, several researchers say. Agriculture is considered essential work under the shelter-in-place orders expanding across the country. But farmers must still adhere to social-distancing requirements and can be buffeted by regulations and other changes along the food supply chain, such as the shuttering of restaurants.

Some work can easily continue with little interruption. For example, many U.S. farmers producing staple crops, including wheat and rice, do so with mechanized tools that already limit human-to-human contact and fall within the Centers for Disease Control and Prevention guidelines for limiting the spread of the coronavirus. The nonprofit International Food Policy Research Institute (IFPRI) reported earlier this month that COVID-19 does not currently pose major threats to overall global food security because adequate stores of staples remain available.

But higher-value and more specialized crops face a greater number of hurdles, says Will Martin, a senior research fellow at IFPRI and a co-author of the report. These foods—such as some fruits and organic produce grown by smaller-scale farms—generally require more labor. They are also often sold to restaurants and farmers markets, many of which are now widely closed or have reduced service across the country, rather than directly to the grocery stores that are still operating. Even if these farmers are able to continue working, they may have limited places to sell their goods. "That's a big problem," Martin says. Higher-value goods are also more likely than major staple crops to experience a price spike caused by COVID-19 disruptions, according to the United Nations Food and Agriculture Organization.

The situation is to be expected in a pandemic, Martin says, citing a 2006 World Bank report that outlines how efforts to contain such outbreaks–including restaurant closures and disruptions to public transportation and tourism–tend to take a larger toll on the global economy than the hours of work lost from people falling ill. The report estimated that a modern pandemic similar to the 1918 Spanish flu would result in a 0.9 percent loss in GDP because of sick workers, compared with a 1.9 percent loss linked to policies enforced to control infection. Farmers of high-value crops get hit especially hard by those policies, Martin says.

One example comes from apple orchards, which require large crews to plant and prune trees. Pruning helps eliminate diseased branches and gives foliage more access to sunlight. But many apple growers rely on seasonal workers from outside of the country for these tasks, and many of these workers are struggling to get visas processed because of embassy and federal office closures. Without an adequate workforce, growers may have to leave trees unplanted and branches unpruned. This neglect could lead to losses later this season and in future years, says Diane Kurrle, senior vice president of the USApple Association, a nonprofit organization based in Falls Church, Va., that represents growers and others in the industry.

Strawberries are another crop likely to be affected, though for different reasons. California strawberry growers do not rely as heavily on a workforce from outside of the U.S., but laborers would typically congregate more closely than is advised to prevent the spread of the virus. Mark Bolda, a University of California Cooperative Extension farm adviser based in Watsonville, says farmers he has spoken to in the surrounding county–where roughly 40 percent of the state's strawberries sold fresh are produced–have already begun making plans to spread workers between rows.

Strawberries, however, hit prime ripeness within a narrow window of just two to three days and must be picked quickly, Bolda says. Spacing workers this way may slow picking, which could lead to more fruit being left to rot in the fields. This situation could, in turn, slow the harvest process even further as workers pause to remove old fruit so rot does not spread to ripening berries. Such a slowdown would reduce the amount of fruit picked per hour that workers were paid for and could hurt a farmer's profits, Bolda says. "Being slower is expensive."

In Maine, growers of lowbush blueberries–the state's highest-grossing crop after potatoes–are currently preparing for their annual import of roughly 50,000 beehives, which arrive on flatbeds from around the country during the spring bloom in April and May. Blueberries rely heavily on bees to transfer pollen, because their narrow flowers are not well adapted for wind pollination. Native bee populations are not substantial enough to support the state's roughly 3,800 acres of lowbush blueberry fields. So growers rent honeybee hives to boost their yields in the nation's second-largest commercial pollination event after one devoted to California almonds, says Lily Calderwood, a wild blueberry specialist at the University of Maine Cooperative Extension.

But transporting hives on flatbeds requires special training, notes Maine beekeeper Lincoln Sennett, who owns a honey business and leases his bees for blueberry pollination. If truck drivers fall ill with COVID-19, beekeepers may struggle to find capable substitutes. Going without these hives could take a serious toll on this year's blueberry yield. "It would be very bad," Calderwood says, noting that a single hive can increase yields by up to 1,000 pounds.

As COVID-19 leads to widespread income losses, fewer consumers may be able to afford specialized or high-value products, including organic vegetables, notes Megan Konar, a civil and environmental engineer at the University of Illinois at Urbana-Champaign. Reductions in such purchases could further stress growers, especially if they sell directly to consumers at markets rather than through grocery stores. "This is an interesting extreme event to food systems, because it's really just a social event," she explains. "There's no weather shock or infrastructure failure or shortcoming." Natural disasters tend to only impact a particular area–a hurricane may wipe out crops in Florida, for example–but the coronavirus has had a much more pervasive effect on a social and institutional level. "It's a bit of a different sort of disaster than normal," Konar says.

If additional environmental stressors do arise this season–such as the river flooding from snowmelt and spring rains anticipated in the Midwest–the industry will become yet more vulnerable, Konar adds. "Whenever you bombard the agricultural sector with simultaneous hazards, it accumulates," she says. "It all adds up and makes it a harder season."

How to Make the Food System More Energy Efficient

By Michael E. Webber

For more than 50 years, fossil fuels and fertilizers have been the key ingredients in much greater global food production and distribution. The food-energy relationship has been a good one, but it is now entering a new era. Food production is rising sharply, requiring more carbon-based fuels and nitrogen-based fertilizers, both of which exacerbate global warming, river and ocean pollution, and a host of other ills. At the same time, many nations are grappling with how to reduce energy demand, especially demand for fossil fuels.

Although transportation, power plants and buildings receive a lot of policy attention as targets for reducing energy consumption, our food supply is often overlooked. In the U.S., about 10 percent of the energy budget goes to producing, distributing, processing, preparing and preserving the plant and animal matter we consume. That is a considerable wedge of the energy pie.

Examining our food supply through the lens of energy use reveals opportunities for smart policies, innovative technologies and new dietary choices that can potentially solve food and energy problems together. The same steps would also make our bodies, and our ecosystems, healthier.

Farm to Fork Is Highly Inefficient

Simple math shows that food production is an inefficient process. Plant growth is not energy-efficient: photosynthesis typically converts less than 2 percent of incoming solar energy into stored energy. That low rate is worsened when animals convert plant matter into beef (5 to 10 percent efficiency) or chicken (10 to 15 percent). We then ingest that food and convert it into human energy stored as glycogen in muscles and as fats–notably around our midsection.

Given the abundance of photons striking the earth every day, low efficiencies hardly seem to matter. But when faced with limits on land, fresh¬water, fertilizer runoff, and fossil-fuel affordability and emissions, the inefficiencies can be daunting. The energy used to make food is vastly greater than the amount of energy we get out of it. The U.S. expends roughly 10 units of fossil energy to produce one unit of food energy.

The magnitude of consumption is remarkable when one considers the entire population. A healthy, active adult male's nominal instantaneous power consumption is approximately 125 watts. That equates to roughly 2,500 nutritional calories per day, or about 10,000 British thermal units (Btu). Thus, the 312 million people in the U.S. need about one quadrillion Btu (one quad) of food energy every year. Because we use 10 units of fossil energy to produce one unit of food energy, feeding the population requires 10 quads–which is 10 percent of the total annual U.S. energy consumption of 100 quads. If we as a society wish to reduce our food-energy consumption, we need to find ways to reduce the 10:1 ratio of energy input to food output.

The food energy needed to feed the world's seven billion people is about 25 quads a year, which is only about 5 percent of the world's 500 quads of annual consumption. It is not that the rest of the world is more efficient than the U.S. Rather one billion people are hungry, another billion are at risk of hunger and many more simply do not consume much.

Extensive energy use has dramatically increased food production through innovations such as diesel powered tractors, electric irrigation pumps, and fertilizers and pesticides made from natural gas and petroleum. Since the mid-20th century crop yields from this green revolution have gone through the roof, and we have transformed deserts such as the Central Valley of California into the world's fruit baskets. At the same time, the percentage of workers needed for agriculture has plummeted.

Cheap energy, primarily petroleum, has also created transportation networks that have improved food distribution significantly, bringing us unexpected fare such as salads and fresh oranges in the middle of winter from far-flung corners of the globe. We expend more energy still to preserve and prepare our food.

When fossil-fuel prices were low and we did not care much about pollution or emissions, we did not worry about the energy waste. Now that prices are higher and we care more about environmental impacts, we have to improve that 10:1 ratio. The inefficiency could get even worse in the U.S. as more people, powered by cheap air conditioning, move into areas where local food production can support a mere fraction of the growing population (think Phoenix). In these cases, even more energy is used either to bring inferior lands into production through energy-intensive fertilizers and irrigation or to move food from remote markets.

Global trends will aggravate the challenge. World population is projected to grow to more than nine billion by 2050. Per capita energy and food consumption will rise, too: notably, as people get richer, they consume more meat, which is much more energy-intensive than other foods. And climate change implies that food production will be hurt by crop losses from droughts and floods, saltwater intrusion into aquifers, higher temperatures (which will decrease the effectiveness of photosynthesis in many places) and competition from biofuels for farmland. As a consequence, experts predict that food production will have to double by 2050.

Local Farming Might Not Help

Unfortunately, thinking about some popular food production "solutions" through the lens of energy shows that they do not always help. For example, many people have latched onto the local-food movement, billing themselves "locavores," as an antidote to the energy used to transport food long distances and the energy intensity of large-scale industrialized agriculture. "Eat local" campaigns encourage residents to shop for local food from farmer's markets or nearby community-supported farms.

Spending our money in the local community rather than sending it far away can be economically valuable, and having a vibrant local-food system creates resiliency in the event of unexpected occurrences such as war or drought. Local farms, however, sometimes use marginal lands to produce nonnative crops that require more chemicals and more energy for irrigation, and they still get low yields. Strangely enough, shipping food thousands of miles can sometimes require less energy, emit less carbon dioxide and do less environmental damage.

For example, it is typically less energy-intensive to grow lamb in New Zealand, where the animals graze on rain-fed grass that grows mostly without fertilizer or irrigation, and ship it to the U.K. than it is to grow lamb in the U.K. using energy-intensive inputs. Further, large industrialized farms, outfitted with laser-leveled fields (to minimize water losses and fertilizer runoff) and GPS-equipped tractors (to optimize fuel use and crop density) and planted with genetically modified crops designed to use minimal water can be surprisingly resource-efficient when compared with a bunch of distributed farms that inefficiently use energy and water but are closer to home. A Stanford University study concluded that Big Agriculture has spared a lot of carbon emissions because of its yield improvements and economies of scale.

Vertical, urban farms or algae production for feed, now in prototype stages, also has the potential for even greater biomass production per square foot of land than local farms.

Some popular solutions for renewable energy actually complicate the food-energy system. Food-based feedstocks–corn, soy, sugar and palm–dominate the world markets for biofuels and create unhealthy competition for farmland and freshwater. In 2010 in the U.S., about 30 million acres–more than one fourth of overall corn production–were used to produce 12.7 billion gallons of ethanol. That share will rise significantly as the U.S.

tries to meet the federal mandate that 20 percent of all liquid transportation fuel come from biofuels by 2022.

Exploit the Waste

Despite all the concerns of the food-energy nexus, there is some cause for optimism. With different innovations, policies, markets and cultural choices that focus on reducing waste and inefficiencies, we can reduce the 10:1 ratio of energy used to energy eaten, as well as mitigate environmental damage.

A first step is to stop using corn kernels for starch-based ethanol, which is the current U.S. practice. Let us use the kernels to feed people and livestock and use only the cellulosic stover (the stalk and leaves of the plant) to make ethanol or synthetic fuels. U.S. energy policy already includes a push for this solution. The Energy Independence and Security Act of 2007 has a renewable fuels standard that mandates that we consume 36 billion gallons of biofuels per year by 2022 and that 16 billion of those gallons come from cellulosic sources. The latter requirement is a rare acknowledgment by politicians in Washington, D.C., that corn might not solve all our energy problems; experts predict we can produce only up to 15 billion gallons a year from corn-based feedstocks grown on available farmland without undercutting our ability to feed ourselves.

The aggressive biofuels rollout, however, pushes the food-based forms online the quickest, with cellulosic forms many years behind because they are more difficult to produce. Nature has designed cellulosic materials over many millennia to not break down. Breaking them down for ethanol means we have to reverse nature, which requires enzymes—code for money; producing enzymes at industrial scales is expensive. Nevertheless, we can overcome the technical hurdles and move more strongly in that direction. Using cellulosic sources instead of food-based sources can help the U.S. energy supply and also free up tens of millions of acres for other food production.

Another step to improve the food-energy equation is to convert agricultural waste products into power. Livestock manure is one rich resource. In the old days, small farms had a mix of animals and a variety of crops in one location; farmers spread manure instead of chemical fertilizer on fields of crops. Today, with large farms that grow just a handful of mega crops and with concentrated animal-feeding operations, that closed-loop practice has been lost. The massive amounts of manure created by large animal operations far exceed any local demand, and it is too expensive to ship cross-country to big farms. The system also creates environmental hotspots such as manure lagoons, which are significant emitters of greenhouse gases and sources of toxic waste. The lagoons are remarkably energy dense, however, and there are many of them; U.S. farms generate more than one billion tons of manure annually.

Anaerobic digesters and micro turbines could convert that manure into enough renewable, low-carbon biogas-fired electricity to displace 2.5 percent of the nation's power generation while reducing greenhouse gas emissions. This approach would also yield another revenue stream for farmers. Researchers at leading agricultural institutions such as Texas A&M University and Cornell University College of Agricultural and Life Sciences are looking at new ways to incorporate anaerobic digestion of manure into farm operations. Juehnde, a small German village working with Frank Mitloehner of the University of California, Davis, is generating so much biogas for heating and cooking that the town has become independent from the national gas grid. Policy makers could encourage the installation of more digesters and turbines by giving farmers access to low-cost capital, creating incentives such as property-tax breaks for the equipment, offering information and training sessions so that potential users know how to operate the systems, and establishing net metering–a system allowing any electricity generated on-site to reduce farmers' utility bills.

Another waste stream that can save food energy is carbon dioxide from smokestacks at coal plants. It can be used to grow algae for human food, animal feed and fuel, thereby avoiding some traditional energy inputs for agricultural production. Some people already eat algae directly for nutritional reasons, and some national restaurant chains use them as a stiffening ingredient. Algal lipids can also be converted into biodiesel, providing a low-carbon, domestic, renewable fuel that is made from something other than food-based feedstock. The remainder of the algal biomass is typically made up of proteins and carbohydrates, which might displace corn-based feed for animals, making more corn available for food and thereby contributing positively to the food-energy nexus. Some algae grow well in brackish water or saltwater, too, eliminating demand for freshwater. Private industry (through a variety of start-ups such as Solazyme), national labs such as the National Renewable Energy Laboratory, and universities such as the University of Texas at Austin and the University of California, San Diego, all have active testing and pilot programs. Although algal solutions seem to be decades away from large-scale implementation, their promise warrants additional research, so policy makers should continue funding development.

More Crop per Drop

Simply implementing innovative agricultural techniques that have already been perfected in pilot programs on a much wider scale could significantly reduce the 10:1 energy-food ratio. For example, drip irrigation provides more crop per drop, sparing freshwater and the energy needed to pump it. The conventional approach–the center-pivot sprinklers that create alienlike green crop circles in the middle of brown deserts (easily visible when flying overhead)–is extremely wasteful, spraying water into the air where a major fraction evaporates. Droplets that do land on crops are likely to hit the leaves and stalks instead of the roots, causing more evaporation loss. In a typical drip-irrigation setup, long sections of narrow tubing laid at the bottom of plants sown in a row deliver water directly to the roots. Researchers at Iowa State University estimate that corn farmers in that state would use 40 percent less water and lower their energy bills by 15 percent with drip irrigation. Half a dozen large farm suppliers now offer the systems, which, if used widely, could save thousands of megawatt-hours of electricity nationwide every year. Incentives to switch to drip irrigation, combined with penalties for wasted water, might hasten adoption.

No-till agriculture is another promising approach. It reduces the disturbance of soils by using special planting equipment that places seeds into untilled soil through narrow surface slots rather than the blunt approach of turning the soil. Disturbing the soil less reduces labor, irrigation, energy, erosion and carbon emissions. Argentina is the world leader; more than half the farms there deploy this advanced technique. Training for farmers about the advantages of no-till can be implemented through agricultural extension services nationwide.

Laser-leveled fields can minimize erosion, irrigation and fertilizer runoff. Most fields have a gradual slope, which causes unequal water distribution and uneven collection of runoff. Rather than risking one portion getting less water than it needs, farmers often overfill the entire field, with the excess spilling over into local waterways. By making fields level, farmers waste less energy pumping water, and less fertilizer is needed because less runs off.

The advent of GPS-enabled tractors, combines and other machinery—today a standard feature offered by manufacturers such as John Deere—has introduced the concept of "precision farming," which drives up productivity and drives down energy use. GPS guidance allows farmers to tend fields and plant crops literally to the inch, reducing wasted space, time and fuel, without even needing to steer machines with their hands. Although the upgrades for a moderately sized farm might cost $10,000, researchers at Purdue University have shown that the benefits outweigh the cost. For one thing, fuel use decreases. Incorporating GPS with field diagnostics allows farmers to map out soil conditions and fine-tune the application of chemicals, which can vary from one end of a field to the other, ultimately requiring less. Fields can also be worked at night and during fog and rain, when human visibility is limited, pushing productivity up.

Better Behavior

Reducing wasted food can also lower the 10:1 ratio of energy used to food eaten. An egregious 25 percent or more of the food grown is wasted annually. That massive amount represents 2.5 percent of annual U.S. energy consumption–more energy than all the ethanol produced in 2011 in the U.S. and more than the energy that will be produced in 2030 from lifting drilling restrictions today on the outer continental shelf. Simply decreasing the amount of food we throw away might reduce energy consumption and greenhouse gas emissions more over the next decade or two than many of the expensive or controversial energy supply policies that have been proposed.

Many methods of reducing food waste can begin tomorrow. We can invest in diagnostics that monitor food spoilage instead of using the crude date-based labeling system that has been in place for several decades. One example is temperature- and time-sensitive inks on food packaging that cause labels to change color if the food has been exposed to the wrong temperature for too long. Start-up companies produce these labels, which could spare a lot of food that is unnecessarily thrown away by stores that are worried about making their customers sick. The labels could indeed also prevent a lot of illnesses induced by spoiled food. Requiring companies to keep track of the temperatures that food has been exposed to–in addition to how long the food has been packaged–might give retailers and consumers better information about the risks of spoilage.

Different attitudes and dietary choices can help, too. Restaurants can stop serving mammoth portions, and consumers can stop bragging about their conquests at all-you-can-eat buffets. More extra food can be kept and eaten as leftovers. We can shift our diets to replace at least some of our energy-intensive meats with less energy-intensive fruits, nuts, vegetables, beans and grains. These behaviors do not require invention; they just require new thinking. Many of them end up saving consumers money as well. Having meatless Fridays or veggie Mondays might start to get us there.

As the original green revolution showed, large-scale changes can be implemented relatively quickly over just a few decades. The changes can be dramatic, achieving outcomes far better than anticipated. Yet surprises can arise, too: years of abundant food production have increased the incidence of obesity and aggravated climate change. Technology alone is not enough; even with the original green revolution, hunger has not been solved. A global approach to reducing the energy waste in food that incorporates new behaviors, attitudes and policies will be critical to widespread success. There is no reason to think this new green revolution will be any different.

About the Author

Michael E. Webber is associate director of the Center for International Energy and Environmental Policy and assistant professor of mechanical engineering at the University of Texas at Austin.

Feeding a Hot, Hungry Planet

By Lisa Palmer

We need to move beyond thinking about the environment–our land, water and air–only as a source of inputs for the food system. Instead we need to recognize that global environmental changes can diminish yields, reduce the amount of food we produce, and affect how nutritious it is and where we produce it.

But just how does the experience of change prompt food systems actors and institutions to work toward solutions?

Weather extremes and environmental shocks, for instance, will likely occur more frequently in the future. In California, the multi-year drought and recent lifting of the drought emergency after a heavy rain and snow year has had a cascade of lingering effects, calling for greater management of both extremes and making water conservation "a way of life" by executive order. The four objectives of California's new management plan include educational and policy nudges such as using water more wisely, eliminating water waste, strengthening local drought resilience and water holding capacity, and improving agricultural water use efficiency and drought planning.

Any successful answer to feeding a hot, hungry planet will result from continual changes, shifts, and adaptation to an uncertain future. Figuring out where society can sustainably grow more food and how people might try to do that under climate change will be inextricably linked to national security, public health, and economic goals. Food system challenges in a changing climate have already led to political instability in some places, and migrations and tensions over changing amount and location of natural resources are likely to grow.

Creating sustainable food systems that deliver nutritious food while also satisfying long term food security is a complex undertaking, as I learned over the past few years while writing and researching my new book *Hot, Hungry Planet: The Fight to Stop a Global Food Crisis in the Face of Climate Change*. I met with the people who are working at the issue from every angle. The farmers, agronomists, and researchers I talked with are trying to fulfill economic, social and environmental objectives while not compromising prospects for future generations.

In India, I met with Pravin Bhai Parmar in the village of Dhundi in Gujarat who was developing a solar irrigation cooperative with five other vegetable farmers. The region where he lives has been over pumping groundwater while also experiencing changes in monsoon rains and steadily falling aquifers. On less than two acres, Parmar grows vegetables, rice, millet, and wheat, and rotates his production seasonally. In summer months, roughly June through September, the crops rely on monsoon rains; but during the rest of the year, irrigation is the only way crops can grow.

With pooled resources, farmers in Dhundi installed solar irrigation panels to run their water pumps and signed a 25-year power purchase agreement to sell back surplus to the power utility. Income from excess power can be almost as much as what they earns from a crop. If the farmers only water their plots when truly needed, they can benefit from solar by supplementing their income, while the environment benefits by incentivizing farmers to conserve groundwater.

I saw compelling evidence in Colombia that farmers who were trying to produce more food per acre of land could intensify production sustainably, weather a changing climate, and make the changes pay off remarkably fast. Fabiola Vega, a farmer in the hilly northern Cauca region, had produced coffee for years but high temperatures and more intense and unpredictable rains made it almost impossible to achieve the yields she needed to cover her costs. She switched some of her coffee production to a plantain and coffee mixed system (shade grown coffee), and used the remaining land for dairy production, raising a small herd of cattle in a silvopastoral system by concentrating them in field richly planted with leguminous shrubs.

And in western Uganda, girls and women enrolled in a high school and a women's-only agricultural university that prepares them for rural development and agricultural work are trying to reverse the trend that increasing one's education automatically means a move to an urban area. Based on the notion of land-grant universities in the United States, the university graduates work in rural transformation, and deliver knowledge and practical information to other women, who are the main agricultural producers in their area. The path to high school and university level education acts as a leverage point for women to improve rural employment and agriculture, while building food security, adding value to their families, and developing skills as community leaders.

Feeding the world in the face of environmental uncertainty without degrading the planet is one of the great civilizational challenges of our time. The cascade of effects and relationships across systems are so complex and variable, we need to move beyond a simple story. We need to move beyond thinking about the environment only as a source of inputs into the food systems or the site of impacts from food systems activities. Instead, we must recognize that environmental changes will influence the potential for food systems to contribute to human and environmental health, and that decision by producers, land managers, corporations and consumers to build resilience to withstand extremes of the years to come will pay dividends.

We need everyone at the table. It's time to move beyond the simple story by bringing together the science on environmental dynamics and global change with food systems institutions and agricultural sciences. When climate scientists, agronomists, agribusiness leaders, NGOs and policy makers, and consumers, too, can work together to make sustainability and adaptation a fundamental component of our global food system, we can foster a holistic, solutions-oriented perspective rather than address them as individual crises.

The views expressed are those of the author(s) and are not necessarily those of Scientific American.

About the Author

Lisa Palmer is the author of Hot, Hungry Planet: The Fight to Stop a Global Food Crisis in the Face of Climate Change. *She is a journalist and a senior fellow at the National Socio-Environmental Synthesis Center in Annapolis, Maryland.*

Long Live Microbiomes!

By Louise Maher-Johnson and Ayana Elizabeth Johnson

Food writer Mark Bittman has argued that because food is defined as "a substance that provides nutrition and promotes growth" and poison is a substance "that promotes illness," then "much of what is produced by industrial agriculture is, quite literally, not food but poison." While that may be an extreme statement, our food system is arguably at risk for several reasons, including the increasing use of herbicides and pesticides; the rise of genetically modified organisms (GMOs); and climate change.

Since 1892, the U.S. Department of Agriculture has been collecting data on the nutritional composition of our foods. Over the decades since, there has been enough variability in how samples have been harvested, stored, prepared and analyzed to make it hard to tease out exact trends or causes of them. There is some evidence that vitamin and mineral content of foods such as broccoli has declined and some to the contrary. Given how fundamental nutrition is to our health, it's surprising there is so little robust research on how agricultural practices affect the nutrient content of crops.

But that is changing. Recent studies have shown, for example, that the increase in atmospheric carbon dioxide is accelerating photosynthesis. That may sound like a good thing, but it means that while plants are growing faster, they also contain more carbohydrates but fewer nutrients, which could ultimately lead to worldwide nutrient deficiencies.

In addition, many crops are getting sprayed more and more heavily with pesticides and weed killers. To protect them from the latter, biotechnologists have genetically modified plants to be herbicide-resistant. About 90 percent of the corn grown in the U.S. (our number-one crop) has been altered adding protective genes from other species. These modifications allow corn to be sprayed repeatedly with herbicides including glyphosate (the active ingredient in Monsanto's Roundup, the most used herbicide in the country and likely globally as well), 2,4-D and dicamba. Nature doesn't take this affront lying down, and weeds quickly evolve herbicide resistance, leading to a chemical arms race.

All three of these herbicides are water-soluble, meaning they can dissolve and can go anywhere water goes. They're also systemic (they can get inside plants, so they can't be washed off before eating). Glyphosate, in particular, is ubiquitous. It's an active ingredient in hundreds of products sold in the U.S. and has been found in air, rainwater, drinking water, rivers, and wetlands and in the groundwater used for crop irrigation. And the synergistic effects of these and other pesticides are inadequately tested.

Corn is also engineered with genes that can enable it to produce multiple insecticidal proteins in every cell, which the Environmental Protection Agency euphemistically terms "plant-incorporated protectants." Plus, corn seeds are often coated with neonicotinoids (insecticides that can harm bees, including types associated with colony collapse) and fungicide. This means they don't need to be sprayed with as much pesticide–but whether this is a net benefit for human and animal health is poorly known.

But because corn is an ingredient in so many foods (corn syrups and oils; corn-fed farm animals), we are often ingesting these pesticides and insecticidal proteins in every bite. Modified soy, the number-one genetically modified crop globally, has glyphosate residues and perhaps a less healthy nutritional profile compared with organic soy. More broadly, there is some evidence that exposure to glyphosate can lead to cancer, endocrine issues and other health problems. A group of medical and environmental scientists recently published its strong, collective concerns about the risks and urged more research.

If ever there was a scenario in which to apply the precautionary principle, this is it. As applied to environmental science, wrote David Kriebel of the University of Massachusetts, Lowell, and his colleagues in a 2001 paper, this entails four components: "taking preventive action in the face of uncertainty; shifting the burden of proof to the proponents of an activity; exploring a wide range of alternatives to possibly harmful actions; and increasing public participation in decision making."

In the mid-20th century, the green revolution introduced the wide use of chemical fertilizers and pesticides around the world. And over the past two decades, we've undergone a "gene revolution" in industrial agriculture. Proponents of these two advances claim that the chemical and technological transformation of our food system is necessary to feed the world–but there is reason to be skeptical, especially when two thirds of America's corn crop goes to animal feed or ethanol production. As the United Nations' Human Rights Council put it, "The assertion promoted by the agrochemical industry that pesticides are necessary to achieve food security is not only inaccurate, but dangerously misleading."

And as if the potential health risks from these two revolutions weren't enough, both have relied on the intensive use of fossil fuels for synthesizing agricultural chemicals; running tractors, combines and other farm equipment; processing and precooking food; manufacturing plastic packaging; and powering refrigeration and long-distance transport. As a result, modern agriculture and land use changes are one of the leading causes of climate change.

Do these factors mean a doomsday scenario? Well, maybe. Or they could signal that it's time for a third revolution.

The Microbiome Renaissance

A microbiome is simply a community (or biome) of microorganisms–bacteria, fungi, archaea and protozoa. The microbiome renaissance we envision will include respecting both our internal and external ecosystems, at a microscopic scale but with macro implications.

In soil, microorganisms by the trillions are essential for the growth, nutrition and health of plants. They do everything from fixing nitrogen to delivering minerals and trace elements, to decomposing organic matter and defending against plant diseases. In short, soil microorganisms drive plant productivity–and greater plant diversity results in both more microbial activity and carbon storage.

To reap all these benefits of healthy soil, we must nurture the soil microbiome and plants' own microbiomes. There is a whole highly-connected microbial food web within the soil that intensive industrial agriculture disrupts. Glyphosate has been shown to hinder the beneficial colonization of mycorrhizal fungi on roots, as has GM corn. Conversely, organic practices support a more diverse and robust microbial community and soils with higher microbial biomass, activity and diversity—as well as up to three times more earthworms. As a February 2015 editorial in *Science* put it, we should "give soils their due."

In humans, our 30 trillion or so cells are matched by a similar number of microorganisms, our "inner soil," that function throughout our body in exchange for food and shelter. Our microbiome performs a wide range of critical functions, such as bolstering our immune system, manufacturing vitamins and supporting digestion. (Have you thanked your microbiome today?)

This is why the overuse of antibiotics (more than 800 prescriptions are written each year for every 1,000 people in the U.S.) is a cause for concern: our internal microorganisms, in balance, help keep us healthy, whereas growing antibiotic resistance, fueled in part by overprescription and in part by the indiscriminate use of these drugs in animal feed, is a serious health problem.

The key to this microbiome renaissance will be nurturing rather than killing or disrupting the balance of our friendly and essential microbiota. Achieving this will require humanity to make organic regenerative farming and gardening the status quo. Regenerative farming means working with, not warring against, nature: planting and saving diverse varieties of heritage seeds; protecting pollinators; growing biodiverse crops; using natural fertilizers such as legumes and nitrogen from the atmosphere; recycling organic matter (mulches and composts); utilizing multispecies cover cropping and crop rotations to build soil; and grazing (not confining) farm animals.

Not only is transforming agriculture to regenerative practices a likely win for our health—and for nature more broadly—it can also be a key climate solution. As we've written previously, humanity can sequester carbon and improve nutrition through the regenerative farming of land and sea. This approach can be applied at all scales, including Climate Victory Gardens in yards, local parks, terraces and rooftops.

This is also a food justice issue, because organics are often more expensive and less available in poor communities and communities of color. Hence the importance of efforts to make organic foods available to everyone and of ending huge "farm bill" subsidies to corn and other big commodity crops–and instead subsidizing the transition to regenerative practices.

A 2018 report by the InterAcademy partnership, a global network of more than 100 national and regional science and medicine academies concluded, "living within planetary boundaries (including those for nutrients, water and climate) and having healthy populations requires new approaches to food systems."

It is pure hubris to think we can manipulate nature into agricultural perfection with synthetic fertilizers and pesticides. Instead, to adapt to and mitigate the intertwined ecological, human-health and climate crises, we must respect the elegant complexity of nature. We must overhaul our food system. And it can all start by ensuring that microbiomes flourish.

The views expressed are those of the author(s) and are not necessarily those of Scientific American.

About the Authors

Louise Elizabeth Maher-Johnson is a retired English teacher and current regenerative farmer, who raises heritage chickens at Skyhill Farm, and who raised Ayana.

Ayana Elizabeth Johnson, Ph.D., is a marine biologist, policy expert and Brooklyn native. She is founder of the consultancy Ocean Collectiv and the think tank Urban Ocean Lab. Find her on Twitter @ayanaeliza.

Section 2: Innovations in Food Systems

Growing Skyscrapers: The Rise of Vertical Farms

By Dickson Despommier

Together the world's 6.8 billion people use land equal in size to South America to grow food and raise livestock–an astounding agricultural footprint. And demographers predict the planet will host 9.5 billion people by 2050. Because each of us requires a minimum of 1,500 calories a day, civilization will have to cultivate another Brazil's worth of land–2.1 billion acres–if farming continues to be practiced as it is today. That much new, arable earth simply does not exist. To quote the great American humorist Mark Twain: "Buy land. They're not making it any more."

Agriculture also uses 70 percent of the world's available freshwater for irrigation, rendering it unusable for drinking as a result of contamination with fertilizers, pesticides, herbicides and silt. If current trends continue, safe drinking water will be impossible to come by in certain densely populated regions. Farming involves huge quantities of fossil fuels, too–20 percent of all the gasoline and diesel fuel consumed in the U.S. The resulting greenhouse gas emissions are of course a major concern, but so is the price of food as it becomes linked to the price of fuel, a mechanism that roughly doubled the cost of eating in most places worldwide between 2005 and 2008.

Some agronomists believe that the solution lies in even more intensive industrial farming, carried out by an ever decreasing number of highly mechanized farming consortia that grow crops having higher yields–a result of genetic modification and more powerful agrochemicals. Even if this solution were to be implemented, it is a short-term remedy at best, because the rapid shift in climate continues to rearrange the agricultural landscape, foiling even the most sophisticated strategies. Shortly after the Obama administration took office, Secretary of Energy Steven Chu warned the public that climate change could wipe out farming in California by the end of the century.

What is more, if we continue wholesale deforestation just to generate new farmland, global warming will accelerate at an even more catastrophic rate. And far greater volumes of agricultural runoff could well create enough aquatic "dead zones" to turn most estuaries and even parts of the oceans into barren wastelands.

As if all that were not enough to worry about, foodborne illnesses account for a significant number of deaths worldwide—salmonella, cholera, *Escherichia coli* and shigella, to name just a few. Even more of a problem are life-threatening parasitic infections, such as malaria and schistosomiasis. Furthermore, the common practice of using human feces as a fertilizer in most of Southeast Asia, many parts of Africa, and Central and South America (commercial fertilizers are too expensive) facilitates the spread of parasitic worm infections that afflict 2.5 billion people.

Clearly, radical change is needed. One strategic shift would do away with almost every ill just noted: grow crops indoors, under rigorously controlled conditions, in vertical farms. Plants grown in high-rise buildings erected on now vacant city lots and in large, multistory rooftop greenhouses could produce food year-round using significantly less water, producing little waste, with less risk of infectious diseases, and no need for fossil-fueled machinery or trans¬port from distant rural farms. Vertical farming could revolutionize how we feed ourselves and the rising population to come. Our meals would taste better, too; "locally grown" would become the norm.

The working description I am about to explain might sound outrageous at first. But engineers, urban planners and agronomists who have scrutinized the necessary technologies are convinced that vertical farming is not only feasible but should be tried.

Do No Harm

Growing our food on land that used to be intact forests and prairies is killing the planet, setting up the processes of our own extinction. The minimum requirement should be a variation of the physician's credo: "Do no harm." In this case, do no further harm to the earth. Humans have risen to conquer impossible odds before. From Charles Darwin's time in the mid-1800s and forward, with each Malthusian prediction of the end of the world because of a growing population came a series of technological breakthroughs that bailed us out. Farming machines of all kinds, improved fertilizers and pesticides, plants artificially bred for greater productivity and disease resistance, plus vaccines and drugs for common animal diseases all resulted in more food than the rising population needed to stay alive.

That is until the 1980s, when it became obvious that in many places farming was stressing the land well beyond its capacity to support viable crops. Agrochemicals had destroyed the natural cycles of nutrient renewal that intact ecosystems use to maintain themselves. We must switch to agricultural technologies that are more ecologically sustainable.

As the noted ecologist Howard Odum reportedly observed: "Nature has all the answers, so what is your question?" Mine is: How can we all live well and at the same time allow for ecological repair of the world's ecosystems? Many climate experts–from officials at the United Nations Food and Agriculture Organization to sustainable environmentalist and 2004 Nobel Peace Prize winner Wangari Maathai–agree that allowing farmland to revert to its natural grassy or wooded states is the easiest and most direct way to slow climate change. These landscapes naturally absorb carbon dioxide, the most abundant greenhouse gas, from the ambient air. Leave the land alone and allow it to heal our planet.

Examples abound. The demilitarized zone between South and North Korea, created in 1953 after the Korean War, began as a 2.5-mile-wide strip of severely scarred land but today is lush and vibrant, fully recovered. The once bare corridor separating former

East and West Germany is now verdant. The American dust bowl of the 1930s, left barren by overfarming and drought, is once again a highly productive part of the nation's breadbasket. And all of New England, which was clear-cut at least three times since the 1700s, is home to large tracts of healthy hardwood and boreal forests.

The Vision

For many reasons, then, an increasingly crowded civilization needs an alternative farming method. But are enclosed city skyscrapers a practical option?

Yes, in part because growing food indoors is already becoming commonplace. Three techniques–drip irrigation, aeroponics and hydroponics–have been used successfully around the world. In drip irrigation, plants root in troughs of lightweight, inert material, such as vermiculite, that can be used for years, and small tubes running from plant to plant drip nutrient-laden water precisely at each stem's base, eliminating the vast amount of water wasted in traditional irrigation. In aeroponics, developed in 1982 by K. T. Hubick, then later improved by NASA scientists, plants dangle in air that is infused with water vapor and nutrients, eliminating the need for soil, too.

Agronomist William F. Gericke is credited with developing modern hydroponics in 1929. Plants are held in place so their roots lie in soilless troughs, and water with dissolved nutrients is circulated over them. During World War II, more than eight million pounds of vegetables were produced hydroponically on South Pacific islands for Allied forces there. Today hydroponic greenhouses provide proof of principles for indoor farming: crops can be produced year round, droughts and floods that often ruin entire harvests are avoided, yields are maximized because of ideal growing and ripening conditions, and human pathogens are minimized.

Most important, hydroponics allows the grower to select where to locate the business, without concern for outdoor environmental conditions such as soil, precipitation or temperature profiles. Indoor farming can take place anywhere that adequate water and energy can be supplied. Sizable hydroponic facilities can be found in the U.K., the Netherlands, Denmark, Germany, New Zealand and other countries. One leading example is the 318-acre Eurofresh Farms in the Arizona desert, which produces large quantities of high-quality tomatoes, cucumbers and peppers 12 months a year.

Most of these operations sit in semirural areas, however, where reasonably priced land can be found. Transporting the food for many miles adds cost, consumes fossil fuels, emits carbon dioxide and causes significant spoilage. Moving greenhouse farming into taller structures within city limits can solve these remaining problems. I envision buildings perhaps 30 stories high covering an entire city block. At this scale, vertical farms offer the promise of a truly sustainable urban life: municipal wastewater would be recycled to provide irrigation water, and the remaining solid waste, along with inedible plant matter, would be incinerated to create steam that turns turbines that generate electricity for the farm. With current technology, a wide variety of edible plants can be grown indoors. An adjacent aquaculture center could also raise fish, shrimp and mollusks.

Start-up grants and government-sponsored research centers would be one way to jump-start vertical farming. University partnerships with companies such as Cargill, Monsanto, Archer Daniels Midland and IBM could also fill the bill. Either approach would exploit the enormous talent pool within many agriculture, engineering and architecture schools and lead to prototype farms perhaps five stories tall and one acre in footprint. These facilities could be the "playground" for graduate students, research scientists and engineers to carry out the necessary trial-and-error tests before a fully functional farm emerged. More modest, rooftop operations on apartment complexes, hospitals and schools could be test beds, too. Research installations already exist at many schools, including the University of California, Davis, Pennsylvania State University, Rutgers University, Michigan State University, and schools in Europe and Asia. One of the best known is the University of

Arizona's Controlled Environment Agriculture Center, run by Gene Giacomelli.

Integrating food production into city living is a giant step toward making urban life sustainable. New industries will grow, as will urban jobs never before imagined–nursery attendants, growers and harvesters. And nature will be able to rebound from our insults; traditional farmers would be encouraged to grow grasses and trees, getting paid to sequester carbon. Eventually selective logging would be the norm for an enormous lumber industry, at least throughout the eastern half of the U.S.

Practical Concerns

In recent years I have been speaking regularly about vertical farms, and in most cases, people raise two main practical questions. First, skeptics wonder how the concept can be economically viable, given the often inflated value of properties in cities such as Chicago, London and Paris. Downtown commercial zones might not be affordable, yet every large city has plenty of less desirable sites that often go begging for projects that would bring in much needed revenue.

In New York City, for example, the former Floyd Bennett Field naval base lies fallow. Abandoned in 1972, the 2.1 square miles scream out for use. Another large tract is Governors Island, a 172-acre parcel in New York Harbor that the U.S. government recently returned to the city. An underutilized location smack in the heart of Manhattan is the 33rd Street rail yard. In addition, there are the usual empty lots and condemned buildings scattered throughout the city. Several years ago my graduate students surveyed New York City's five boroughs; they found no fewer than 120 abandoned sites waiting for change, and many would bring a vertical farm to the people who need it most, namely, the underserved inhabitants of the inner city. Countless similar sites exist in cities around the world. And again, rooftops are everywhere.

Simple math sometimes used against the vertical farm concept actually helps to prove its viability. A typical Manhattan block covers about five acres. Critics say a 30-story building would therefore provide only 150 acres, not much compared with large outdoor farms. Yet growing occurs year-round. Lettuce, for example, can be harvested every six weeks, and even a crop as slow to grow as corn or wheat (three to four months from planting to picking) could be harvested three to four times annually. In addition, dwarf corn plants, developed for NASA, take up far less room than ordinary corn and grow to a height of just two or three feet. Dwarf wheat is also small in stature but high in nutritional value. So plants could be packed tighter, doubling yield per acre, and multiple layers of dwarf crops could be grown per floor. "Stacker" plant holders are already used for certain hydroponic crops.

Combining these factors in a rough calculation, let us say that each floor of a vertical farm offers four growing seasons, double the plant density, and two layers per floor–a multiplying factor of 16 (4 × 2 × 2). A 30-story building covering one city block could therefore produce 2,400 acres of food (30 stories × 5 acres × 16) a year. Similarly, a one-acre roof atop a hospital or school, planted at only one story, could yield 16 acres of victuals for the commissary inside. Of course, growing could be further accelerated with 24-hour lighting, but do not count on that for now.

Other factors amplify this number. Every year droughts and floods ruin entire counties of crops, particularly in the American Midwest. Furthermore, studies show that 30 percent of what is harvested is lost to spoilage and infestation during storage and transport, most of which would be eliminated in city farms because food would be sold virtually in real time and on location as a consequence of plentiful demand. And do not forget that we will have largely eliminated the mega insults of outdoor farming: fertilizer runoff, fossil-fuel emissions, and loss of trees and grasslands.

The second question I often receive involves the economics of supplying energy and water to a large vertical farm. In this regard, location is everything (surprise, surprise). Vertical farms in Iceland, Italy, New Zealand, southern California and some parts of East Africa would take advantage of abundant geothermal energy. Sun-filled desert environments (the American Southwest, the Middle East, many parts of Central Asia) would actually use two- or three-story structures perhaps 50 to 100 yards wide but miles long, to maximize natural sunlight for growing and photovoltaics for power. Regions gifted with steady winds (most coastal zones, the Midwest) would capture that energy. In all places, the plant waste from harvested crops would be incinerated to create electricity or be converted to biofuel.

One resource that routinely gets overlooked is very valuable as well; in fact, communities spend enormous amounts of energy and money just trying to get rid of it safely. I am referring to liquid municipal waste, commonly known as blackwater. New York City occupants produce one billion gallons of wastewater every day. The city spends enormous sums to cleanse it and then dumps the resulting "gray water" into the Hudson River. Instead that water could irrigate vertical farms. Meanwhile the solid by-products, rich in energy, could be incinerated as well. One typical half-pound bowel movement contains 300 kilocalories of energy when incinerated in a bomb calorimeter. Extrapolating to New York's eight million people, it is theoretically possible to derive as much as 100 million kilowatt-hours of electricity a year from bodily wastes alone, enough to run four, 30-story farms. If this material can be converted into useful water and energy, city living can become much more efficient.

Upfront investment costs will be high, as experimenters learn how to best integrate the various systems needed. That expense is why smaller prototypes must be built first, as they are for any new application of technologies. Onsite renewable energy production should not prove more costly than the use of expensive fossil fuel for big rigs that plow, plant and harvest crops (and emit volumes of pollutants and greenhouse gases). Until we gain operational experience, it will be difficult to predict how profitable a vertical farm could be. The other goal, of course, is for the produce to be less expensive than current supermarket prices, which should be attainable largely because locally grown food does not need to be shipped very far.

Desire

It has been five years since I first posted some rough thoughts and sketches about vertical farms on a Web site I cobbled together (www.verticalfarm.com). Since then, architects, engineers, designers and mainstream organizations have increasingly taken note. Today many developers, investors, mayors and city planners have become advocates and have indicated a strong desire to actually build a prototype high-rise farm. I have been approached by planners in New York City, Portland, Ore., Los Angeles, Las Vegas, Seattle, Surrey, B.C., Toronto, Paris, Bangalore, Dubai, Abu Dhabi, Incheon, Shanghai and Beijing. The Illinois Institute of Technology is now crafting a detailed plan for Chicago.

All these people realize that something must be done soon if we are to establish a reliable food supply for the next generation. They ask tough questions regarding cost, return on investment, energy and water use, and potential crop yields. They worry about structural girders corroding over time from humidity, power to pump water and air everywhere, and economies of scale. Detailed answers will require a huge input from engineers, architects, indoor agronomists and businesspeople. Perhaps budding engineers and economists would like to get these estimations started.

Because of the Web site, the vertical farm initiative is now in the hands of the public. Its success or failure is a function only of those who build the prototype farms and how much time and effort they apply. The infamous Biosphere 2 closed-ecosystem project outside Tucson, Ariz., first inhabited by eight people in 1991, is the best example of an approach not to take. It was too large of a building, with no validated pilot projects and a total unawareness about how much oxygen the curing cement of the massive foundation would absorb. (The University of Arizona now has the rights to reexamine the structure's potential.)

If vertical farming is to succeed, planners must avoid the mistakes of this and other nonscientific misadventures. The news is promising. According to leading experts in ecoengineering such as Peter Head, who is director of global planning at Arup, an international design and engineering firm based in London, no new technologies are needed to build a large, efficient urban vertical farm. Many enthusiasts have asked: "What are we waiting for?" I have no good answer for them.

About the Author

Dickson Despommier is professor of public health and microbiology at Columbia University and president of the Vertical Farm Project, which functions as a clearinghouse for development work (see www.verticalfarm.com). As a postdoctoral fellow at the Rockefeller University years ago, he became friends with René Dubos, a renowned agricultural sciences researcher who introduced him to the concept of human ecology.

The Future of Farming

By Andrew Sharpley

Phosphorus, a nutrient essential to crop growth, may have been the first element to be chemically discovered, but it is one of the most difficult to track. This is especially true when it comes to nutrient management on farms.

Deficiencies in plants are hard to spot, and the phosphorus cycle through soil and watersheds is a delicate balance susceptible to human influence, while losses to the environment are coming under increasing scrutiny.

Scientists have made great strides in understanding phosphorus in the lab, and in recent years, we have made significant progress in helping farmers in the field to better understand how to cost-effectively use phosphorus fertilizer to address and avoid losses.

But a wider dissemination of this knowledge is vital for ensuring the sustainable use of phosphate fertilizers to help farmers rise to the challenge of food production.

We know that phosphorus deposits are finite, making it important that we conserve and recycle phosphorus for future generations. Ensuring that the tools and technologies developed across the fertilizer sector are available to farmers to help them meet their productivity goals while minimizing environmental footprint is also paramount.

I have been very fortunate to have worked with and benefited from many scientists with different expertise during my career, which has helped broaden the impact of our research. When we can translate and share this with those who need it, such as farmers, the impact can be far-reaching.

One such example is the development of the P Index, a tool that helps farmers identify which areas on their farm are more susceptible to phosphorus nutrient loss. Using the P Index is helping to reduce the amount of phosphorus lost to the environment in the U.S., an estimated 25,000 tons.

The success of the P Index is demonstrated by the fact that in 49 states, the Natural Resources Conservation Service (NCRS) has adopted it as the cornerstone of nutrient management planning at Concentrated Animal Feeding Operations, or CAFOs. This approach is also used by the Environmental Protection Agency (EPA) to cost-effectively prioritize and target conservation measures across the US.

Another example of applied nutrient management studies is the research and demonstration Arkansas Discovery Farm Program.

Across the 12 farms, researchers are evaluating how to minimize the potential movement of nutrients from land into water to protect soil and reduce nutrient runoff. This includes evaluating the effectiveness of conservation methods, such as reduced tillage and cover crops, alongside nutrient management best practices.

Program findings so far have shown that less than five and three per cent of applied nitrogen and phosphate fertilizers are lost annually in surface run-off on average. Computerized planning tools have also helped improve irrigation water management, reducing irrigation runoff to less than 10 per cent of current common losses and saving one of the most precious commodities to many farmers.

Initial program results have already given farmers proof and confidence that they are providing safe and affordable food supplies, while protecting natural resources for future generations. Seeing the practices in action has also empowered them to further improve their nutrient management and water conservation.

Most importantly, these experiential learning programs show farmers what works, provides a powerful vehicle for them to influence future agricultural policy, and enables them to be proactively invested in both food and environmental security.

Finally, the 4R Nutrient Stewardship is a fertilizer industry–led lab-to-land initiative that promotes efficient fertilizer use. The initiative encourages farmers to apply the "Right" nutrient source, at the "Right" rate, at the "Right" time and in the "Right" place.

When used with other conservation measures, it can improve soil health in addition to improving crop yields and reducing losses to water. The 4R Plus project in Iowa, for instance, is designed to reduce nitrogen and phosphorus losses to water by at least 45 per cent.

Supporting scientific research into nutrient cycle management and its transfer to farmers is key for enabling more sustainable farming. Improvements in nutrient and soil management not only give an economic boost for farmers, by allowing them to grow more crops with fewer inputs, but also strengthen food security and environmental sustainability for all of us.

The views expressed are those of the author(s) and are not necessarily those of Scientific American.

About the Author

Andrew Sharpley, PhD, is winner of the 2019 IFA Norman Borlaug Award and professor in the Department of Crop Soil and Environmental Sciences at the University of Arkansas.

Agroecology Is the Solution to World Hunger

By Raj Patel

Although it is the sharp edge of the battle to end hunger, you could be forgiven for thinking you were watching a reality TV cooking show. Under the low peak of Bwabwa Mountain in Malawi, in a village on a tributary of the Rukuru River, about 100 people gather around pots and stoves. Children crowd around a large mortar, snickering at their fathers', uncles' and neighbors' ham-fisted attempts to pound soybeans into soy milk. At another station, a village elder is being schooled by a man half his age in the virtues of sweet potato doughnuts. At yet another, a woman teaches a neighbor how he might turn sorghum into a nutritious porridge. Supervising it all, with the skill of a chef, the energy of a children's entertainer and the resolve of a sergeant, is community organizer Anita Chitaya. After helping one group with a millet sponge loaf, she moves to share a tip about how mashed soy and red beans can be turned into patties by the eager young hands of children who would typically never volunteer to eat beans.

There is an air of playful competition. Indeed, it is a competition. At the end of the afternoon the food is shared, and there are prizes for both the best-tasting food (the doughnuts win hands down) and the food most likely to be added to folks' everyday diets (the porridge triumphs because although everyone likes deep-fried food, doughnuts are a pain to cook, and the oil is very expensive).

This is a Recipe Day in Bwabwa, a village of around 800 people in northern Malawi. These festivals are sociological experiments to reduce domestic inequality and are part of a multifaceted approach to ending hunger called agroecology. Academics describe it as a science, a practice and a social movement. Agroecology applies ecology and social science to the creation and management of sustainable food systems and involves 10 or more interconnected principles, ranging from the maintenance of soil health and biodiversity to the increase of gender and intergenerational equity. More than eight million farmer groups around the world are experimenting with it and finding that compared with conventional agriculture, agroecology is able to sequester more carbon in the soil, use water more frugally, reduce dependence on external inputs by recycling nutrients such as nitrogen and phosphorus, and promote, rather than ravage, biodiversity in the soil and on farms. And on every continent, research shows that farmers who adopt agroecology have greater food security, higher incomes, better health and lower levels of indebtedness.

Chitaya told me that at the turn of the millennium, when Bwabwa's farmers were still practicing conventional agriculture, "there were times when we wouldn't be able to eat for days. My first child was malnourished." Now her oldest son, France, is a very healthy adolescent, helping teach other boys how to cook. The pediatric malnutrition clinic near Bwabwa has closed down for want of cases–though in Malawi as a whole, more than a third of the children younger than five years are stunted by malnutrition. Despite the COVID-19 pandemic, whose devastating economic effects have deepened malnutrition across the world, agroecology continues to help Bwabwa evade hunger.

Yet when policy makers attend a United Nations Food Systems Summit in the fall of 2021, the solutions on the table for world hunger will exclude agroecology. The summit's sponsors include the Gates Foundation, whose preferred solution is a set of technologies modeled on the Green Revolution. Despite a great deal of evidence that the Gates' Alliance for a Green Revolution in Africa has failed, one of its leading acolytes from Rwanda will chair the U.N. Summit. Advocates for agroecology, such as the Alliance for Food Sovereignty in Africa, which represents 200 million food producers and consumers, have too few resources to impact a process that increasingly silences their voices.

Ending hunger requires much more than pulling more food from the ground; it involves grappling with entrenched hierarchies of power. Over the past decade food production has generally outstripped demand–there is more food per person than there ever was. But because of global and regional inequalities, exacerbated by the recent pandemic, levels of hunger are higher now than in 2010. In other words, more food has accompanied more hunger. People are deprived of food not because it is scarce but because they lack the power to access it.

The global food system was originally established under colonialism, when the agriculture and land-ownership patterns of much of the tropical world were reconfigured, and tens of millions of enslaved and bonded laborers were shipped around the world to provide Europeans with cane sugar and other tropical crops for which they had developed a taste. Far from ending with colonialism, however, this system of food extraction has grown only stronger because of conditions attached to loans from international financial institutions such as the World Bank and the International Monetary Fund (IMF). To pay its debts, Africa now exports everything from roses to broth.

Agroecology frees the world's poorest farmers from such structures of control and shifts the balance of power in the global food system to people like Chitaya, one of billions who reside at the very bottom of the socioeconomic pyramid. Little wonder, then, that it is unpopular with conventional agricultural businesses, governments in the Global North and the organizers of the food systems summit. Its recognition that systemic problems require systemic solutions makes agroecology a threat.

Hunger in Malawi

Over a lifetime of trying to get to the bottom of why there is hunger and what might be done about it, I have traveled from within organizations like the U.N. and the World Bank to protest lines outside and within the World Trade Organization. During the past decade, however, I have also had a scientific education at the hands of some of the world's poorest farmers.

My first visit to Bwabwa was in 2011, at the invitation of my graduate school friend Rachel Bezner Kerr. Now a professor of development studies at Cornell University, Bezner Kerr had arrived in Malawi a decade earlier to find herself in the middle of an economic crisis. Malawi had suddenly reduced fertilizer subsidies—and that, too, while the HIV/AIDS pandemic was wreaking humanitarian and economic havoc. Farmers, most of whom practiced industrial agriculture, which requires expensive chemical inputs, were desperate. Bezner Kerr wanted to be of service as she developed a project for a master's degree, so she sought the most disadvantaged families to support in her research. She was lucky to meet Esther Lupafya, a nurse who headed the maternal and child health program at a clinic in the small town of Ekwendeni. Together they identified farmers, including Chitaya, who were ready to try a different kind of agriculture—one that would free them from dependence on global agrobusiness and its allies.

Getting to Bwabwa involves a six-hour drive north from Malawi's capital, Lilongwe. Lined with signs heralding the projects of several nongovernmental organizations and foreign aid institutions, the northern road from the Lilongwe airport tracks the eastern shore of Lake Malawi, the continent's third-largest freshwater lake. After passing northern Malawi's biggest city, Mzuzu, with its six-story Bank of Malawi Building, and the smaller town of Ekwendeni, you follow dirt roads to reach Bwabwa. Whereas the large, flat, irrigated fields off the main highway are neat monocultures of corn, the fields near the village are drier, smaller, canted at every angle and packed with twirling thickets of different crops, each tailored to the needs of the family tending it and the capacity of that particular field's ecology.

Northern Malawi did not always look like this. The first white man to visit was Scottish Presbyterian David Livingstone in 1858. His missionary campaign led to the establishment of the British Central African Protectorate, which later became Nyasaland. Photographs from the time show scrubland. British agriculturist B. E. Lilley gazed on Malawi in the 1920s and declared: "The time has not arrived when the native can be looked to as a person who can be relied upon to raise produce to anything [like] the extent that the white man raises it." Similar attitudes persist to this day, though they are now couched in contemporary language.

Keen to wring what they could from the colony's resources, the British began to export ivory and forest products, moving on to the crops that would transform Malawi's land and economy: tea, cotton, sugar and tobacco. The colonists took over the land, but they needed workers, so they imposed a hut tax, an annual household fee payable in cash. Initially families paid the colonists by selling their stores of wealth, usually livestock, until there was nothing left to liquidate. Then they sent able-bodied men to sell their labor, in Malawian plantations and the mines farther south. Debt turned self-sufficient farmers and pastoralists into manual workers, laboring for a pittance.

Debt also turned Malawi into a pawn of its creditors. Malawi became independent in 1964, only to spend the next 30 years under autocrat Hastings Banda. Western donors rewarded his iron-fisted regime with high-dollar loans to support the country's industrial development while ignoring its worsening malnutrition. Such loans became the instruments of Malawi's, and in fact Africa's, hunger. In the early postcolonial period, Africa was a net food exporter, selling 1.3 million tons a year from 1966 to 1970. But the oil-price crisis of the 1970s forced African governments to borrow even more from the World Bank and the IMF. These so-called structural adjustment loans came with strict conditions that, among other measures, slashed public spending on education and health care and privatized national assets. Further, African countries were instructed to concentrate on exports of the colonial-era crops, which would earn the dollars with which they might repay their debts.

Despite paying an average of $100 million per year to its creditors throughout the 1980s, however, Malawi remains one of the most indebted countries on Earth. Worse, devoting the richest land to growing cash crops for export, instead of food crops for subsistence, meant that structural adjustments had by the 1990s turned Africa into an importer of a quarter of its food. Between

2016 and 2018 Africa imported 85 percent of its food from outside the continent–a debilitating dependence.

Trial, Review, Exchange

In 1992 a national survey revealed that 55 percent of Malawian children had failed to reach the appropriate height for their age–a key measure of malnutrition. The government tried to defy the austerity imposed by international banks and donors by subsidizing fertilizers for farmers but eventually caved to their demands to instead prioritize paying off the loans. Lupafya and Bezner Kerr began their work soon after these supports were removed, establishing the Soils, Food and Healthy Communities (SFHC) initiative in Ekwendeni in 2000. Starting with 30 farmers, the SFHC now works with more than 6,000 people across 200 villages to promote agroecology.

Along with Chitaya and others, the women began with a round of experiments, intercropping local groundnuts and other legumes. This double-legume system allowed the farmers to harvest nuts and beans for their children and then dig the nitrogen-rich residue back into the soil to boost maize production–without buying fertilizer. Some farmers went further, experimenting with vegetable intercropping patterns. Simultaneously, the SFHC developed a system of peer review, in which the participants met regularly to discuss measures to improve soil fertility. Women farmers had long been exchanging seeds and knowledge to grow finger millet, a drought-tolerant plant that produces highly nutritious grains that make for hearty porridge and, if you can stomach it, sour beer. The SFHC formalized this tradition of evaluating and sharing information.

By running trials of different legume cropping systems in a "mother" location in the middle of different villages, farmers could then adopt "baby" trials in their own fields based on their preferences for soil health, nutrition and the time they could spare to tend the crops. Through discussions and iterations over the years, initial trials grew from a few dozen households to reach thousands of farmers, with a pigeon-pea-and-groundnut combination proving to be the most successful in fixing nitrogen. As the soil improved, some farmers, many of them women, did well enough not only to feed their families but also to sell a respectable surplus at the local market.

Still, every farmer, every field and every season are different, so the experiments continued. Some women tried seemingly incongruous combinations such as soy and tomatoes–originating in Asia and the Americas, respectively–alongside indigenous African varieties such as finger millet. (Millet cultivation had earlier been discouraged because the grain could not be exported for dollars, but it persisted because women often brew it into beer as a means of earning extra income.) In Bwabwa, the fields are a mixture of foreign and native varieties, selected through trial and observation, with networks of farmers exchanging knowledge and ideas and reviewing one another's work.

That openness to experimentation and adaptation explains why, around March, it is possible to see in the unpromising red soil a cultivation system that looks like it may not belong. Tall rows of corn burst from the ground. Twirling around them are pole beans, and at their feet are the fat, dark fan-shaped leaves of local pumpkin, together with their blossoms. In Mesoamerican agriculture, this kind of technique is known as the three sisters: corn, beans and squash.

In Malawi, locally adapted varieties work together in similar ways: the corn or millet provides the starchy cereal that forms the backbone of every meal. The stalks also scaffold the beans, which yield protein and fix nitrogen. Root nodules in legumes (such as beans and groundnuts) are a site of symbiosis between the plant and rhizobia bacteria. The plant provides the bacteria with energy; the bacteria take nonreactive nitrogen molecules from the air and turn them into ammonia and amino acids for the host. This works well for cereals, which need bioavailable nitrogen to do well. The pumpkin (or other squash) provides big leaves for shading out weeds, and its flowers attract beneficial insects that keep pest pressure down. Plus, at the end of the season, there are gourds.

What Is Agroecology?

Agroecology is a way of producing food that mimics nature, using biodiversity and the recycling of resources and nutrients to increase productivity, control pests, eliminate chemical inputs and enrich soils. Just as important, it enables marginalized communities not only to produce enough food for themselves and others in a sustainable way but also to ensure that it is distributed fairly, enhancing nutrition and gender, intergenerational and other forms of equity. The U.N.'s Food and Agriculture Organization has identified 10 key principles that communities pursuing agroecology follow.

Synergies
The various subsystems of agroecology work together synergistically to create something that is far greater than the sum of its parts. Agroecology not only reduces hunger and poverty, it preserves and enhances soil fertility, water supply, nature, culture and community for the benefit of present and future generations, delivering justice and equity to marginalized people.

Human and Social Values
Attention to equity, inclusion and justice ensures that no one goes hungry. Women, who in most cultures are responsible for feeding the family, are among the key innovators and leaders of agroecology projects. Whereas industrial systems devalue farm labor, food production becomes an enjoyable, shared task and a vehicle for enhancing ties with nature and the community. Protecting the environment enables future generations to inherit intact natural systems.

Culture and Food Traditions
Industrial agriculture and global trade have generated imbalanced diets worldwide, with cardiovascular diseases and diabetes existing in tandem with starvation and malnutrition. Agroecology allows local food cultures to thrive, restoring a direct relation between food production and consumption.

Recycling
Agroecology recycles natural resources and nutrients. Like nature, it produces no waste. In recurring cycles, atmospheric nitrogen moves into the soil and back, rainwater travels from grove to field to air, manure from farm animals provides fertilizer and crop residues such as straw become livestock feed.

Efficiency
Half the nitrogen provided by synthetic fertilizers ends up polluting the environment, while thirsty hybrid or genetically modified crops deplete water tables. In contrast, agro-ecological systems use resources and nutrients with optimal efficiency. Locally adapted seeds, water harvesting, nitrogen-fixing microbes and natural predators help produce food with minimal external inputs.

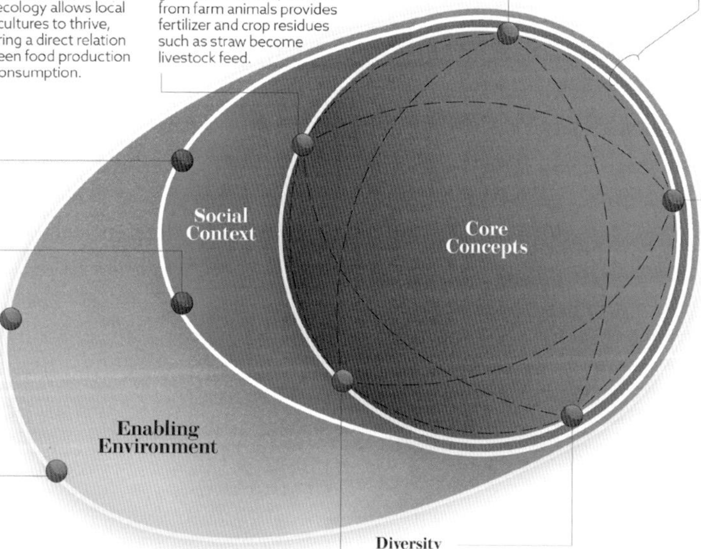

Resilience
Crop diversity ensures quicker recovery from climate-related disasters and other natural exigencies. In addition, the ability to grow food with local and recycled inputs helps to insulate communities from external economic shocks.

Diversity
Intercropping diverse species increases productivity and resilience—one crop might fail in conditions that enable another to thrive. Enhancing biodiversity, by providing habitats for frogs, birds and other predators, for example, helps to control pests. Moreover, agro-ecological systems are themselves diverse, each being tailored to local ecology and culture.

Responsible Governance
Systems of governance at global, national and local levels that protect the rights of food-growing communities to land, clean water, intellectual property (such as traditional seeds and know-how) and other resources are essential for agroecological systems to thrive. Existing systems of trade and governance militate against the well-being of small farmers, who are among the hungriest and most indebted people in the world.

Co-creation and Sharing of Knowledge
Communities work together to identify and share the agroecological practices that fit best with their particular ecological and cultural circumstances. There is no universal, top-down prescription of what should be grown and how; instead there are guidelines for a process of shared experimentation and discovery that lead to different solutions in different places.

Circular and Solidarity Economy
Agroecology seeks to link producers and consumers of food in local circles, so that production is directly tied to need. Such localized economies boost the incomes of food producers, provide consumers with fresher produce, foster community ties, and reduce food waste and energy use in transportation.

Credit: Federica Fragapane; Source: The 10 Elements of Agroecology: Guiding the Transition to Sustainable Food and Agricultural Systems, Food and Agriculture Organization of the United Nations, 2018 (reference)

When put together, these crops produce more food per unit area than when they grow alone. Polycultures are demonstrably more abundant than monocultures. After harvest, the crop residue is reincorporated into the soil to build fertility and structure for the soil's biome.

In the early 2000s, as soil fertility in Bwabwa improved, some of the poorest women began to harvest an abundance of cereal, beans and vegetables. Interest in the cropping techniques spread. But despite real improvements in food production, child malnutrition remained puzzlingly high. Some of the farmers in the project, excited that they were becoming agronomists, started to wonder how to tackle the problem more directly. As they would discover, they had made progress in freeing themselves from external structures of power–but had yet to tackle internal ones.

Wrestling Down Patriarchy

Through her work at the pediatric clinic, Lupafya had formed a suspicion: tradition was partly to blame for infant malnutrition. Ethnographic research across the SFHC villages confirmed her hunch. Within the patriarchal extended family, mothers-in-law have authority over their daughters-in-law. When an ill-founded parenting tip–that children cry because they are not being given solid food–is propagated through these networks, young mothers often find themselves counseled to wean their children at the age of two months. This advice runs counter to overwhelming scientific evidence that exclusive breastfeeding for six months and then a mix of breast and solid food until two years of age offer children the best start in life.

Lupafya crafted a way to walk the tightrope of respectful disagreement. The SFHC trained village women and men as facilitators to broker difficult conversations, particularly those between mothers- and daughters-in-law. Through monthly meetings and leadership from Lupafya and others, the science spread, and the misinformation was dispelled.

Lupafya learned something as well. "Change begins with denial," she told me. "It is the one who debates the most who will change." Having tackled the availability of food and breastfeeding practices, the grassroots social scientists moved to another determinant of infant malnutrition they had identified: domestic violence and, more broadly, patriarchy. Women's autonomy is linked with improved child nutrition indicators. As they observed, gender inequality meant that mothers had to spend time cooking, cleaning, managing the farm and breastfeeding. To have men help in domestic labor would increase women's autonomy. The question was: How do you get men to cook?

To find out how this transformative change happened, I worked with the SFHC team for more than a decade, documenting Chitaya's work in a film called *The Ants & the Grasshopper*. Chitaya had first met Lupafya when she visited the pediatric nutrition clinic. The older woman, Mama Lupafya as she is called, had supported her in a difficult marriage, one into which Chitaya had been coerced. Through attending workshops hosted by the SFHC, then by finding work as one of its trainers, and through long and difficult work in her home, Chitaya has transformed her marriage into one characterized by equality.

There are times when her husband, Christopher Nyoni, struggles to pull his weight in the house. He is afflicted by night blindness, a possible consequence of his own malnutrition early in life. When it gets dark, he is no longer able to cook or clean and needs help finding his way around the house. But by the light of day, he can be seen hunched over a stove or doing laundry or fetching water–all of which are traditionally women's work. It is a sign of Chitaya's success that Nyoni is keen to break with patriarchal tradition: "I do not want my son to get married the way I did," he told me.

The pathway to transforming this and other gender relationships in Bwabwa lay through changing the culture around food. An initial effort to achieve this shift involved door-to-door organizing. Members of the SFHC would visit households with an expert and offer to teach men how to cook novel foods, such as soy. After an enthusiastic afternoon gathered around a stove, surrounded by exhortations to do better, the men promised they would change. They did not. So the SFHC farmers brainstormed an alternative.

A constant worry for men was the social stigma of doing the effeminate work of cooking. "What if my friends see me?" asked Winston Zgambo. Having tried to cater to men's embarrassment by offering private cooking lessons, the SFHC team tried the opposite. They held public cooking competitions for whole families. On Recipe Days, all men were involved in cooking–and it was fun. By gamifying the change in behavior through offering prizes and social recognition for success, the women cracked open the possibilities for changing not just food culture, but inequalities in power within the home.

Data from the SFHC's work speak for themselves. Participation in the program moved children from being below the average weight for their age to surpassing the average. A recent study in which women farmers showed other mothers how to farm led to a range of benefits, from increased dietary diversity for children to lower maternal depression rates and higher rates of fathers' participation in chores.

A Teeming Future

Agroecology means taking care not just of all humans but also of the ecosystems on which we depend. Under chemical agriculture, farmers grow a single crop. They buy fertilizers, pesticides, herbicides and access to water, and if necessary, they rent pollinators to maximize the yield. They use the revenue from selling the harvest to pay their bills and debts. In agroecology, farmers find ways not to exterminate pests but to reach an ecological equilibrium. They accept a little crop loss while providing habitats for predators and introducing other forms of biological control to obtain a much more robust and resilient ecosystem. In northern Malawi, biodiversity is part of the SFHC's success, as it is in every successful agroecological system. There are more insects, amphibians, reptiles, fish, birds and mammals in these landscapes than in the barren green deserts of modern monoculture.

In a world of extreme weather, agroecological diversity–both social and biological–is a source of resilience. When Hurricane Ike ploughed through Cuba in September 2008, it left trees and debris littering the fields. In Sancti Spíritus province, researchers noticed that the farms that followed the principles of conventional agriculture, with vast expanses of the same kind of crop, took around six months to recover from the devastation. But the most diversified farms, with tall plantains, fruit trees, perennial crops and ground cover, were able to recover 80 percent of their prestorm capacity in just two months. With high canopy trees blown over, more light fell on other plants in the understory, which grew faster: the diversity constituted a kind of botanical insurance portfolio. Moreover, families living on diversified farms could save some trees the morning after the storm, when conventional farm workers were far from the fields where their labor was seasonally contracted.

Agroecology also enables income resilience. Small farmers typically receive very little support. Instead they need to manage the flows of cash around the farm themselves. Conventional agriculture has one big burst of cash at harvest time, which may or may not be enough to pay off farming-related debts and dwindles throughout the year. With agroecology, on the other hand, income streams can be augmented by means of crops that mature in the leanest times. In Mexico, for instance, one group of farmers supplements its corn income with countercyclical honey and coffee harvests.

In the absence of reliable banks, farmers have sometimes turned to creating their own circular economies and exchanges. Many places have local grain stores that help to manage the booms and busts in harvests and hunger. In Bwabwa a few years ago women set up a credit circle to help manage cash flow and to develop other income streams, such as the sale of "climate change stoves," cooking stands that require much less wood than conventional wood-burning methods. A dozen women pooled their resources and took turns borrowing the cash and then repaying it. But the savings circle was wiped out in the IMF-mandated devaluation of the Malawian kwacha (currency) in 2012.

The COVID-19 crisis has made farmers' lives harder. Rising food prices have strained finances, and with resources diverted to emergency mitigation measures so that communities could stay home and stay safe, everyone's life has become harder. Yet agroecological practices appear to have enabled the SFHC's villages to endure the pandemic better than communities outside the project.

Feed the World

What happens in Malawi and among the hundreds of millions of farmers experimenting with new kinds of agroecology matters for the planet. Agroecology offers the ability to do what governments, corporations and aid agencies have failed to do: end hunger. For a while, it might have been easy to respond to agroecology by saying "that's all very nice, but it won't feed the world." But farming families that engage in agroecology have improved indicators of income and nutrition. From Nepal to the Netherlands, when agroecology is not confined to the field but extends into the home with equality and into community networks of exchange and care, farmers are financially and physically better off.

With ideas from the World Economic Forum and with support from the food and chemicals industry, the solutions on the table at the U.N. meeting are far less imaginative. Nor do they go far enough to remedy or even acknowledge the environmental and other harms committed by industrial agriculture. This supposedly scientific method of growing food is one of the largest drivers of climate change. Algae blooms from nitrogen and phosphate pollution are devastating aquatic life. Pristine forests are falling to ranches and plantations. Aquifers are being drained for thirsty cash crops. Fertile soil is turning to sterile dust as synthetic chemicals kill essential microbes, and pesticides are decimating insects on which extended chains of life depend.

This past July the Rockefeller Foundation reported that whereas Americans spent $1.1 trillion on food in 2019, the additional external health, environmental, climate change, biodiversity and economic costs associated with the food industry were $2.1 trillion. That is quite a debt–and one that the industry will never have to pay. The rest of the world shoulders the cost. Yet the firms behind this damage are the ones offering solutions at the summit.

We know how to do better. Agroecology more than fits the bill–not only because the crops grown are more diverse but because the social arrangements that surround them are more cognizant of power. Industrial agriculture's hidden costs are precisely the ones agroecology makes explicit. Its pathways reward the acumen of those on the front lines, support the livelihoods of the poor and protect the biodiversity of the planet. Its researchers and practitioners are already hard at work, teaching and learning from one another.

Such networks of knowledge undo the colonial savior complexes to which many development experts are still tied. Instead, under agroecology, as Chitaya puts it, "women can teach men, Black people can teach white people, the poor can teach the rich." She reflects on the certainties of struggle ahead, particularly as the powerful seem to be doubling down on industrial agriculture. "So much has been lost. But it's never too late to change."

About the Author

Raj Patel is a professor of public affairs at the University of Texas at Austin and a member of the International Panel of Experts on Sustainable Food Systems. His books include Stuffed and Starved *and* The Value of Nothing. *Most recently, he co-directed with Zak Piper the award-winning documentary* The Ants & the Grasshopper.

Test-Tube Burger: Lab-Cultured Meat Passes Taste Test (Sort of)

By Arielle Duhaime-Ross

Sci-fi fans and animal-rights activists alike have been announcing its arrival for decades, but in a world where food scientists are still trying to figure out the best ways to extend the life of cake, it's hard to imagine that meat created in a petri dish might gain a place on our dinner plates anytime soon. Yet, today in London, Mark Post, a vascular physiologist at Maastricht University in the Netherlands, allowed two independent tasters to sample a hamburger patty he had grown in his lab. "It had a familiar mouthfeel," said food writer and journalist Josh Schonwald, after biting into a piece of the cooked meat in front of reporters. "[The difference] is the absence of fat." Both tasters were careful not to comment on whether the burger was "good" or not.

The hamburger was grown in Post's lab using bovine skeletal muscle stem cells, collected from a piece of fresh beef. To do this, the cells were "fed" calf serum and commercially available growth medium to initiate multiplication and prompt them to develop into muscle cells over time. Once they differentiated into muscle cells, they were given simple nutrient sources, such as algae extracts. The scientists also exercised the resulting muscle strands in a bioreactor by affixing them to a soluble sugar scaffold and slowly built tension using doughnut-shaped anchor points–essentially helping the muscle to "bulk up."

The resulting five-ounce burger, cooked by chef Richard McGeown, was made using 20,000 strips of cultured meat–about 40 billion cow cells–and took about three months to produce, "which is faster than [raising] a cow," Post joked. The most impressive number associated with the burger, however, is its $325,000 price tag, donated by Sergey Brin, co-founder of Google.

Post is hopeful that he will one day get the cost down to a more competitive price point. "We have done some calculations where we came up with a $70-per-kilo price tag with the current technology," Post notes. "That gives me sufficient confidence that eventually we can scale [the production] up and make it at a reasonable price." But don't expect to find Post's lab-grown meat on your local supermarket shelf in the near future. The goal of the press conference was to show the world that the technology is available, said Post, who added "to improve it, it will take us probably 10 to 20 years to get it to supermarkets."

To get the burger ready for the London taste test today, Post mixed saffron and beet juice, for color, into the strands of meat. The burger itself was prepared in a traditional manner involving bread crumbs and a binder. The patty was then cooked in front of reporters using sunflower oil and butter, which led the second taster, nutrition scientist Hanni Rützler of Michigan Technological University, to lament the absence of salt and pepper. "[The taste] is close to meat," said Rützler, after chewing the freshly prepared meat. "I thought the consistency would be very different. I thought it would be much softer."

Post did not seem too worried about the tasters' reactions. "I think it's a very good start," he said. "This was just to prove that we can do it. I am very happy about it." Post now hopes to work on improving the flavor by cultivating fat tissue. "A lot of the juiciness and flavor comes from fat," Post noted. "It will take another couple of months before we have that down."

For the Dutch researcher, the main reason for exploring this method of meat production is to provide an answer to the mounting food crisis. According to the World Health Organization, the demand for meat will double over the course of the next 40 years. This is a big problem because more than 70 percent of agricultural land is currently being used for livestock production, leaving little room for crops destined for human consumption. Post also points out that lab-cultured meat will help lower methane production, which contributes to climate change.

Although many questions remain as to how the Post and his two lab technicians will manage to mass-produce the meat at a cost that would give ordinary consumers a reasonable alternative to farm-raised beef, one thing is certain: the meat he is producing is not geared toward vegetarians. "We are catering toward letting beef eaters eat beef in an environmentally friendly and ethical way," he says. "Let the vegetarians stay vegetarians–it's even more environmentally friendly than eating cultured meat."

About the Author

Arielle is a Scientific American *editorial intern. She covers a variety of topics including health, technology and zoology.*

Tweaking Vegetables' Genes Could Make Them Tastier—And You'll Get to Try Them Soon

By Meghan Bartels

Today's Brussels sprouts taste better than you might remember from childhood. It's not that your refined adult palate appreciates them better. Rather a new variety has displaced the original vegetable. You can thank plant breeders for the change. And modern breeders, armed with new gene-editing technology, are looking to replicate Brussels sprouts' reinvention.

In the late 1990s scientists identified specific chemicals, called glucosinolates, that made Brussels sprouts taste bitter. Plant breeders started growing old seeds, previously discarded for producing paltry harvests, to identify tastier versions with lower levels of these compounds. Then they crossed these delicious but low-yield plants with modern, more prolific individuals until they found a descendant that made plenty of tasty sprouts, transforming the once maligned vegetable from a bitter pill into a popular side dish.

But other veggies haven't fared as well. That's because most breeding decisions favor plant traits that matter to vegetable growers, not vegetable eaters. "I'd say disease resistance is probably the major focus these days of most breeding programs because that's what imperils the ability of the farmer to grow the crop," says Harry Klee, a professor emeritus of horticulture at the University of Florida, who specializes in tomatoes. "Quality traits are really completely ignored."

In addition, breeders who focus on consumer crops must navigate the controversy surrounding genetically modified organisms (GMOs). Although all domesticated species now have different genetics than their ancestors, in agriculture, the term GMO refers to a plant that carries genes imported from a completely different species—and these changes are subject to stricter regulation. But newer techniques are allowing breeders to work within the context of a plant's own genome, making tweaks that don't trigger complicated rules.

Flavor is challenging to target because different people have different preferences–plus, even under the best conditions, flavor quality is more complex than something like yield. "We've spent a lot of time and money figuring out what flavor is, and most breeding programs don't have the capacity to measure those things," Klee says.

But interest in prioritizing flavor is starting to build, thanks in part to new genetic technology such as the gene-snipping technique CRISPR and DNA sequencing that is cheap enough to use liberally. "There's never been a better time to be a fruit breeder or a vegetable breeder because we have more tools and techniques," says Susan Brown, an apple breeder at Cornell University.

Some companies are beginning to use those tools to tackle the challenge of developing tastier veggies. One company, Pairwise, is fighting the same compounds that plagued Brussels sprouts: glucosinolates. But this time researchers are modifying salad greens–and they're armed with the science of gene editing.

Although kale, for instance, is particularly healthy, many prefer eating the less bitter romaine or iceberg lettuce. So Pairwise scientists figured out how to use CRISPR to edit a kalelike mustard green to fit that palate. They wanted to turn off the genes that code for an enzyme called myrosinase, which breaks down the glucosinolates and creates bitterness once the leaf is chewed in a diner's mouth. The result is a healthy but less bitter green that the company is marketing this year under the brand Conscious Foods.

This is an example of where flavor-minded gene editing can shine, says Tom Adams, co-founder and CEO of Pairwise. "From a gene-editing perspective, I think where taste comes in is that we can remove things that people don't like," he says. "It's a lot more difficult to think about how you can bring in the really complex, great tastes." To create those more complex tastes, Adams says, traditional breeding is still the best path.

Traditional breeding is the cornerstone of another high-tech flavor effort as well, one that seeks to reverse the ways of thinking that got us to tasteless vegetables in the first place. Instead of growing varieties that can withstand the storage and transportation needs of the agricultural system, a company called Plenty is shrinking the vast distance from the field to the table. Plenty grows its plants in indoor vertical farming facilities closer to consumers, so produce stays fresher, says Nate Storey, the company's co-founder and chief science officer.

When Plenty decided to start with greens, he says, the team grew thousands of traditionally bred varieties in its facilities. Then the researchers adopted only the ones that resulted in the tastiest crops rather than trying to develop new varieties. "There's no need to rebuild a wheel," Storey says of the technique. "We just screen all the wheels that exist and find the ones that work best in our system."

This method does not always succeed, however. The company couldn't find a tomato that thrived in its facilities, so it's working on developing its own variety using a sped-up version of traditional breeding.

Tomatoes are a popular target. A third company is creating more flavorful tomatoes using epigenetics–changing the expression of genes instead of the genes themselves. Whereas Pairwise is snipping out the gene sequences that produce an enzyme that interferes with flavor, Sound Agriculture is programming gene expression. This approach dials down production of undesirable compounds by making their genetic sequences less accessible for transcription.

Understanding how precisely to modify expression to get a desired result is still a work in progress, says Travis Bayer, co-founder and chief technology officer of Sound Agriculture. "The science of epigenetics in plants is really exciting and it's something that is evolving pretty rapidly," he says. The company's first epigenetically grown product, a tomato dubbed Summer Swell, is due to hit shelves this spring. Other projects in the works focus on leafy greens, as well as a handful of fruits, Bayer says.

All these vegetable growers hope that more flavorful products on store shelves will convince people to consume the recommended allowances of fruits and vegetables–and do so better than decades of nutritional guidance have.

"Don't waste your time talking about trying to educate people to eat better," says Klee, the tomato breeding researcher. "Just give them products that taste better, that they want to eat."

About the Author

Meghan Bartels is a science journalist and news reporter for Scientific American *who is based in New York City.*

Faux Fish Might Help Aquaculture Keep Feeding the World

By Leslie Nemo

Of the 160 million tons of seafood that end up on people's plates each year, 50 percent comes from aquaculture. Growing all that salmon, tilapia and shrimp requires a steady supply of the perfect food supplement: oily anchovies and sardines, often called forage fish, which are rich in proteins, fats and vitamins. About 90 percent of the 20 million tons of forage fish pulled from the wild each year is ground into meal or oil to nurture fish farmed for human consumption.

But with expectations aquaculture will continue to boom—the United Nations predicts production to increase by 34 percent by 2026—the industry is outgrowing its feed supply. This dilemma has spurred researchers to try to synthesize a stand-in that will provide the nutrients found in forage fish, be economically viable, yet not deplete resources such as grains that humans directly depend on for food. "Fish meal is important in aquaculture, and if [aquaculture] wants to grow, it has to break out of forage fish dependency," says Michael Tlusty, an associate professor of sustainability and food systems at the University of Massachusetts Boston. But "how do you come up with totally new products" to fill this need?

Even at current aquaculture production levels, high demand and limited supplies have made fish meal and oil too expensive to use for more than about 30 percent of a farmed fish's diet. That amount provides enough of the necessary mix of nutrients (including coveted omega-3 fatty acids) to help some species grow faster and thus require less feed overall, says Halley E. Froehlich, a soon-to-be assistant professor at the University of California, Santa Barbara, who studies global aquaculture and fisheries. Most producers fill in the remaining calories with soy, grain and other cheap products.

But soy and grain are already under pressure to supply food for other farmed animals such as cows and pigs—and to directly sustain humans—says Jillian Fry, a seafood and public health researcher at the Johns Hopkins Center for a Livable Future at Johns Hopkins University. Rising demand for such crops is already driving deforestation and overloading waters with fertilizer runoff.

With all this in mind, researchers and start-ups are developing novel feeds from other resources. Some labs are looking to mimic forage fish by reaching one step back in the food web to the algae forage fish themselves eat, and that are the source of those prized omega-3's and other micronutrients. Pallab Sarker, an associate research professor of sustainable aquaculture at the University of California, Santa Cruz, and his team found Nile tilapia gain more weight on less feed—and contain more omega-3's—when they consume a particular algal species instead of the usual fish oil; this suggests algae could be a viable replacement fish fatty acid source for this species of farmed fish. Research in other labs suggests similar microorganisms could substitute a portion of fish products fed to red drum and Atlantic salmon.

Algae are not the only alternate organisms researchers are looking at. Margareth Øverland, a professor with Foods of Norway at the of the Norwegian University of Life Sciences, is testing whether a particular protein-rich yeast, grown on Norwegian spruce wood and seaweed sugars, could be an ersatz fish feed. "The yeast is sustainable because it can be produced independent of arable land, uses little fresh water and can use low-value biomass" for which humans have little food use, she says. Atlantic salmon that had a third of their diet converted to this yeast gained weight as fast as their conventionally fed counterparts, Øverland and her team found. To make the product easier for fish to digest, the researchers are tinkering with their yeast strain and the combinations of sugar they feed it to see if that helps it go down fish gullets more smoothly.

Other researchers are experimenting with everything from bacteria to crickets as forage fish substitutes. Some, although not Sarker or Øverland, are competing in a contest called the

F3 Challenge to see who can sell as much of their oil substitute as possible in an effort to push innovation, Tlusty says.

For most researchers, scaling up presents the biggest hurdle. Replacing the 22 million tons of wild aquaculture fish used every year will require massive volumes of microalgae production. "Our lab can't meet the quantity we'd need to meet feed levels," Sarker says. That production level is also required to drop the price, because otherwise farmers will still opt for the adequate and cheap grain, he adds. He hopes to reach these goals by using by-products from other companies that harvest algae for human dietary supplements and other goods. "This one product will help the micro-algae industry to grow with another stream of revenue," he says.

Inherent to the problem of ramping up production of these feed substitutes is nailing the right ratios of fatty acids, such as omega-3's. Mimicking the natural balance found in fish oil requires one of two methods: Researchers must either find the perfect algal or yeast strains and feed it the right starter, so associated microbes produce everything in proportion–or they must combine fatty acids from various sources, which makes coordinating production even more difficult.

Even if that delicate balance of nutrients can be reproduced, and algae or yeast scaled up to the needed levels, questions remain–such as how much greenhouse gas the imitation feed refinery processes will emit. These feed ideas are still so young it is hard to do the math on that, Tlusty says, though current industrial fermentation processes, like beer brewing, hint at what emissions could look like.

Overcoming the various hurdles and answering those questions may be crucial to maintaining human food-production systems without adding to the mounting pressures on marine ecosystems from overfishing and climate change. "Aquaculture is producing more," Tlusty says, "and we need to make sure as a responsible industry we have all future scenarios mapped out."

About the Author

Leslie Nemo is a freelance science journalist living in Brooklyn, N.Y. You can find more of her work at www.leslienemo.com.

Spray-On, Rinse-Off Food 'Wrapper' Can Cut Plastic Packaging

By Sam Jones

Packaging is essential for preserving and distributing many kinds of foods, but it often incorporates plastic–scraps of which already litter too much of the planet, posing a threat to wildlife and contaminating drinking water and soil. Now researchers say they have developed a nontoxic, biodegradable and antimicrobial food coating that could reduce food waste and foodborne illness without adding plastic to the environment. A new study shows this material can be effectively sprayed on individual pieces of produce, such as fruits or vegetables. Removing it is as simple as rinsing it off with water.

Protecting edible items from bacteria and other microorganisms reduces spoilage, which is a major factor in food being tossed out. And this kind of waste is a root cause of worldwide hunger: every year roughly one third of food produced across the globe goes to waste. That's not the only reason to shield produce from germs–some microorganisms are also the sources of illnesses, including listeriosis and *Escherichia coli* poisoning. Foodborne illnesses cause more than 420,000 estimated deaths worldwide annually.

Unfortunately, packing food to preserve it also adds massively to environmental plastic. "Food packaging is definitely enemy number one when it comes to plastic pollution," says Win Cowger, an environmental scientist at the Moore Institute for Plastic Pollution Research, who was not involved in the new study. "We can see globally that food packaging is the most abundant plastic material in the environment." Although the new coating would only replace a portion of the packaging out there–it would not touch some of the greatest offenders, such as water bottles and coffee cup lids–Cowger says any step toward reducing plastic pollution is a good one.

Plastics can stick around in the environment for a long time—potentially forever—but the new coating is biodegradable. That's because of its primary ingredient: pullulan, an edible fiber that is "generally recognized as safe" (GRAS) by the U.S. Food and Drug Administration. The coating also incorporates the naturally derived antimicrobial agents citric acid and thyme oil, as well as a bacterially produced compound called nisin, all of which are widely deemed safe for human consumption in the amounts involved. It is described in a new study published this week in *Nature Food*.

The study researchers used a manufacturing system called focused rotary jet spinning, or FRJS, to generate antimicrobial-laced fibers and apply them to food. Harvard University bioengineer and study co-author Huibin Chang compares the FRJS system to a cotton candy machine, which rapidly spins melted sugar to drive it through small holes, producing fine strands that can be wrapped around a paper cone. FRJS also creates a focused stream of gossamer fibers (made of pullulan in this case rather than flavored sugar) that can be wrapped around a food item—an avocado, for instance. But FRJS—developed in study co-author and bioengineer Kit Parker's Harvard lab, where Chang is a researcher—was not originally designed for food applications. "When we created this technology, we used it for tissue engineering," Chang says. For example, he explains, FRJS played a role in his previous work building three-dimensional models of certain heart structures.

The researchers tested the coating on avocados because these fruits are especially prone to uneven ripening and postharvest decay. After being deposited on an avocado via FRJS, the nontoxic pullulan coating could be easily rinsed off in a sink and washed down the drain, the study found. "You can package the avocado at the farm and extend the shelf life, and then you can wash the coating away," says study co-author Philip Demokritou, a nanoaerosol researcher at Rutgers University and Harvard. Even if the treated object itself is discarded, its coating will degrade in soil in about three days, according to the scientists.

The team also tested how much the coating improved food safety. When the researchers pitted it against common foodborne pathogens, including *E. coli*, *Listeria innocua* and *Aspergillus fumigatus*, they saw a reduction in both bacterial and fungal populations. They also found that avocados with the coating were less likely to rot: just 50 percent of these fruits went bad over the course of a week, compared with 90 percent of the uncoated produce. And the coated avocados were more likely to retain their green internal color.

Although this is not the first antimicrobial food coating, the researchers believe they have created the most effective and easily disposed of option to date. They contend that the spray-on technology requires less starting material, making it more efficient than silk-fiber-based coatings, which require that food first be dipped in the material and then dried. Other attempts at plastic-free food packaging have involved cellulose-based films; these cannot be rinsed off and some even need to be recycled.

The team is currently working on scaling up the coating process to treat multiple pieces of produce at once, Chang says. The scientists are considering several options, including an assembly-line-based system, but this is still in the early stages of planning.

The coating may also need to undergo further safety testing, suggests Nishad Jayasundara, an environmental toxicologist at Duke University, who was not involved with the study. "As a toxicologist," he says, "the primary thought whenever you see a newly synthesized product is 'Do we know enough about it?'" For instance, although the coating's starting materials are nontoxic, washing them down the drain could make them break down into unexpected by-products.

Jayasundara says he is generally encouraged by the new study results. "It's always very exciting when you have biodegradable material that can replace or reduce plastics at any level possible," he says. But he is hesitant to celebrate just yet. Although the FDA has given pullulan the agency's GRAS designation, Jayasundara cautions that whenever there are modifications to a material—even with natural additives such as the antimicrobials the researchers used–it is important to evaluate their safety to human health using a range of tests.

"When we first thought about plastics, they were deemed pretty safe molecules," Jayasundara notes. "But over time we realized, 'Oh, actually, no, that's not the case.' Now we know that plastics at all levels, regardless of the size, have cellular-level effects, molecular-level effects and ecosystem-level effects."

About the Author

Sam Jones is a biomedical scientist turned science writer, editor and producer based in Washington, D.C.

Advanced Food Tracking and Packaging Will Save Lives and Cut Waste

By Rona Chandrawati and Bernard S. Meyerson

About 600 million people suffer food poisoning every year, according to the World Health Organization, and 420,000 die. When an outbreak occurs, investigators can spend days or weeks tracking its source. Meanwhile more people can sicken, and massive amounts of uncontaminated food may be discarded along with the tainted items. Finding the source can be slow work because food travels a complex path from farm to table, and the records of those journeys are kept in local systems that often do not communicate with one another.

Together a pair of technologies could reduce both food poisoning and food waste. The first, an innovative application of blockchain technology (better known for managing virtual currency), is beginning to solve the traceability problem. Enhanced food packaging, meanwhile, is providing new ways to determine whether foods have been stored at proper temperatures and whether they might have begun to spoil.

Blockchain is a decentralized accounting system in which entries are recorded in sequence in multiple identical "ledgers" stored on computers in multiple locations. This redundancy makes tampering with any one ledger futile, creating a highly trusted record of transactions. A blockchain-based cloud platform developed for the food industry–IBM Food Trust–is already employed by major food sellers. (One of us–Meyerson–is affiliated with IBM.)

By integrating growers, distributors and retailers on a common blockchain, Food Trust creates a trusted record of a given food's path through the end-to-end supply chain. In a test using the technology, Walmart traced the origin of a "contaminated" item in seconds; with the standard mix of written and digital records, this would have taken days. With this capability, retailers and restaurants can remove a contaminated item from circulation virtually immediately and destroy only stock that came from the same source (say, a particular grower of romaine lettuce) instead of wasting entire national stocks of the item. Many food-business giants–Walmart, Carrefour, Sam's Club, Albertsons Companies, Smithfield Foods, BeefChain, Wakefern Food (ShopRite's parent) and Topco Associates (a group purchasing organization)–have joined the IBM Food Trust. Other organizations have also introduced blockchain technology for enhancing traceability.

To prevent food poisoning in the first place, research laboratories and companies are developing small sensors that can monitor the quality and safety of food in pallets, cases or individually wrapped products. For instance, Timestrip UK and Vitsab International have independently created sensor tags that change color if a product has been exposed to above-recommended temperatures, and Insignia Technologies sells a sensor that slowly changes color after a package has been opened and indicates when the time has come to toss the food. (The color changes more quickly if the product is not stored at the proper temperature.) Sensors that reveal the gaseous by-products of spoilage are also being developed. Beyond preventing sickness, such sensors can reduce waste by showing that a food is safe to eat.

Cost remains a roadblock to the ubiquitous use of sensors. Still, the food industry's need to ensure food safety and limit waste is propelling this technology and blockchain forward.

About the Authors

Rona Chandrawati is a senior lecturer and head of the Nanotechnology for Food and Medicine Laboratory at the University of New South Wales (UNSW Sydney) in Australia. Her research focuses on developing colorimetric nanosensors for disease diagnosis, food safety and environmental monitoring. She was a 2018 World Economic Forum's Young Scientist and is in the Forum's Expert Network. She has also served on the World Economic Forum's Global Future Council on Biotechnology (2018–2019).

Bernard S. Meyerson, Steering Group vice chair, is chief innovation officer emeritus at IBM. He is a member of the U.S. National Academy of Engineering and a recipient of numerous awards for work spanning physics, engineering and business. He was the 2014–2016 chair of the World Economic Forum's Meta-Council on Emerging Technologies and the 2016–2018 chair of the Forum's Global Future Council on Advanced Materials. He remains engaged with several WEF efforts, such as "The Future of US Manufacturing" and "Innovation with a Purpose: Strengthening Food Systems through Technology."

Section 3: Controversy Surrounding Food Systems

Organically Speaking: The Marketing Language of Organic Food

By Layla Eplett

Foods themselves might *be* a mouthful but the accompanying language used to describe foods can *say* a mouthful. Guy Cook, an applied linguist and Professor of Language in Education at King's College, explains, "We are influenced by what is said about food offered to us, as much as by the food itself." Part of his research has explored the influence of language in the marketing of organic food.

In 1973, about fifty self-described hippie farmers in Santa Cruz started the California Certified Organic Farmers. It was the first organic certification program in the United States and was perceived to be the embodiment of a counter-culture movement. During the 1980s, organic food expanded from being solely counter-cuisine to encompass what some organic farmers describe as 'yuppie chow'.

In *Fast food/organic food: Reflexive tastes and the making of 'yuppie chow'*, Julie Guthman observes, "It was a young woman from Berkeley who forged the unlikely connection between this early culinary history, the 1960s' counter-culture, and the *nouveau riche* of the 1980s." At her acclaimed restaurant, Chez Panisse, Alice Waters emphasized the use of fresh, locally sourced, seasonal ingredients. One of the ingredients featured at Chez Panisse was organic baby greens. They were acquired from self-proclaimed hippie farmer Warren Weber, who opted to call the greens by the French term *mesclun*. On the menu, Waters included the adjective "organic" to describe the *mesclun*. Though it may not have been conscious or even intentional, Guthman explains that Waters' choice to use the term as a modifier institutionalized a certain set of meanings for organic.

Consumers and producers of organic food has continued to evolve over time. In recent years, large corporations have joined the smaller farms and independent producers more closely associated with the image of organic foods. Sometimes described as Big Food meets Big Organic, companies including Coca-Cola, Kraft, General Mills, PepsiCo, and ConAgra are all capitalizing off the trend and making their own products labeled as organic.

How has the growth and changes in the organic food market been reflected in their marketing language? Cook, along with Matt Reed and Alison Twiner, examined the language used to promote organic food in Great Britain. Over one year, they researched the thoughts of those who designed it and the public's response using a combination of techniques including corpus analysis, focus group discussions, and interviews.

As part of their project, the researchers analyzed the packaging. For example, they examined organic baby new potatoes produced by Tesco, one of the largest grocery and retail stores in the United Kingdom. They found the label included sensual and tactile imagery, alliterative language like "specially selective" and vague claims such as stating they "work with nature." The label also included a picturesque and pastoral image of a rolling green countryside that seemed to be more evocative of England than the potatoes' stated place of origin, Egypt.

Organic labels also often included a narrative of production, using a farmer's name and other information about their farms. Through a corpus comparison of words on packaging on both organic and non-organic products, the researchers also noted that keywords on non-organic products tended to incorporate imagery associated with the kitchen, whereas organic foods emphasized farms and the point of production.

It was unclear whether the promotional strategies of larger corporations influenced the smaller producers or vice versa. Either way, the researchers found, "Whether produced by supermarkets, small politically committed producers, or environmentalist campaign groups, the language used tends to be poetic, vague, dialogic, narrative, and emotive, with an emphasis upon bucolic imagery and consumer self-interest."

Interviews with persons responsible for writing text accompanying organic products revealed there was an assumption that the consumers were more emotional than rational and more interested in "feeling" than fact. Despite this, the study found consumers may not be as easily manipulated as may have been believed. Focus group discussions with individuals from diverse ages, socio-economic statuses and backgrounds indicated there may be a critical resistance to marketing language overall, also that the participants were did not fully trust supermarkets in general (or organic alternatives) and indicated a sense of fatalism and cynicism about the food chain.

The views expressed are those of the author(s) and are not necessarily those of Scientific American.

About the Author

Layla Eplett writes about the anthropology of food. She has a Masters in Social Anthropology of Development from the University of London's School of Oriental and African Studies and loves getting a taste of all kinds of culture–gastronomic, traditional, and sometimes accidentally, bacterial. Find her at Fare Trade.

Does the World Need GM Foods?

By Sasha Nemecek

Yes – *Robert B. Horsch, vice president of international development partnerships at Monsanto Company, received the 1998 National Medal of Technology for his pioneering experiments in the genetic modification of plant cells. He talks about the promise of GM crops.*

Q: How did you become interested in the genetic modification of plants?

A: I started in this field with a strong interest in plants but with what you might call an academic interest in agriculture. I had this vague, naive notion that if we could genetically improve plants with the new tools of molecular biology, we would find a way to make biotechnology relevant to agriculture.

That has now happened. Biotechnology is a great tool that will allow us to produce more food on less land and with less depletion or damage to water resources and biodiversity. I am convinced that biotechnology is not just relevant but imperative for helping us meet the rapidly growing demand for food and other agricultural products. The combination of more people and rising incomes will increase the demand for food by at least 50 percent in the next 25 years.

Q: But critics of genetically modified foods point out that companies are not going to start giving products away. Can a corporation like Monsanto make biotechnology affordable for farmers in the developing world?

A: Cultivating commercial markets and applying technology to help the developing world are not mutually exclusive at all. One approach that works very well is to segment the market into different areas. One is the pure commercial market. It makes economic sense, as a for-profit company, for us to invest in products and market developments in places where we can sell our products and where we think we can make a profit. In 2005 more than 90 percent of the 8.5 million farmers who grew biotech crops were small farmers in developing countries. Commercial expansion has been more successful in developing countries than I would have predicted just a few years ago.

Then there's another area, what I call a transitional market, where we have less experience related to biotechnology but that in the long run I think may be more powerful and beneficial for development efforts. We have used this approach with our older, nonbiotech products, such as high-yielding corn hybrids, and I think we can use it in the future with biotech products. Small farmers can see results in a demonstration plot and, if they want, try it themselves on a portion of their farm. If it works for them, they can expand or repeat it the next year. We have programs like this in Mexico, India and parts of Africa. By the third or fourth year, if it's working, the farmers will have made enough money from the experimentation phase to be able to run essentially on their own.

Q: And what about profits for Monsanto?

A: We sell the seeds and the herbicide at market prices, and we subsidize the learning, the testing and the development of distribution channels so that we don't actually make a profit in the first several years. Only if the project is successful enough to become self-sustaining will we start making a profit. As of 2006, our cooperative development projects in Mexico, India and South Africa have successfully transitioned to self-sustaining markets for Monsanto and for farmers. In sub-Saharan Africa, the products are working well in farmers' hands, but the regulatory capacity and market infrastructure are developing more slowly and still need cooperative help.

Q: Let's turn to the environmental effects of GM crops. What do you consider the most important benefits of the technology?

A: Lower use of pesticides is the environmental benefit that people relate to immediately, and it's huge for a product like Bt cotton. *[Editors' note: Bt crops have been genetically modified to produce a bacterial protein that kills certain insect pests.]* According to a recent report, 380 million pounds of pesticides were not used in the U.S. between 1996 and 2004 as a result of insect-protected crops, and many, many more won't be used in the future as biotech expands in acreage and in traits.

Beyond that there are also yield benefits. The Bt corn we have today doesn't displace a whole lot of insecticides, but what it does do is boost the yields by a noticeable margin. It depends on the year and on the region, but the increase in yield can range from 5 to 15 percent. You get a greater corn harvest with the same resources that you were going to use anyway.

Getting more from really good farmland, then setting aside land that is of marginal quality and returning it to habitat for wildlife is very beneficial to the environment. We can't continue to indefinitely expand our old practices–of chemical use, of water diversion, of plowing wild lands and converting them to farms, of nonagricultural sprawl, and of the production of industrial waste.

Q: One of the benefits of biotech that we first heard about was nutritionally enhanced foods. But despite promises of healthier broccoli, we have Bt corn. The famous "golden rice" is not available to consumers yet and is still in the early stages of testing. Will we ever have nutritionally enhanced foods?

A: We're seeing progress across industry, academia and the non-profit community. Efforts are under way to modify fatty acids to make vegetable oils more healthy for consumers. Monsanto and other companies have commercialized healthier oils derived from conventional breeding and are on track to commercialize improved biotech oils early in the next decade. These healthier oils are designed to produce foods with very low levels of saturated fats. Further research involves ways to produce food crops enriched with omega-3 fatty acids beginning early next decade. These products, including a biotech oilseed, would provide consumers with additional ways to improve heart health. The goal of this project is to create an affordable, land-based, renewable oil source with properties that make it easier to create great-tasting food products than current alternatives.

Efforts to produce nutritional enhancements from biotechnology have been ongoing. But more work is under way at a scale that should lead to success. For instance, the global initiative known as Harvest Plus is using both conventional breeding and biotechnology to increase levels of iron, zinc and vitamin A in beans, cassava, maize, rice, sweet potatoes and wheat.

Q: Monsanto has been one of the most criticized, even despised, corporations because of its role in the development of genetically modified foods. Has it ever been hard to tell people you're an employee of Monsanto?

A: I've had a few people react negatively, but my experience is that when people meet you as a person, their reactions are very different than when they are commenting on the big nameless, faceless company.

I think the company is making an effort to address people's concerns about GM foods more openly. We've recognized that some genetic modifications are particularly bothersome. Among vegetarians, for instance, the idea of eating a vegetable that has an animal gene in it might raise questions. For certain cultures or religious groups, there could be similar concerns. So we decided it was better to avoid using animal genes in food crops.

I don't think it serves anybody's interest–including Monsanto's–to discount the potential risks of biotechnology. But for where we are today, and for what I see in the pipeline for the next few years, I really don't see a measurable risk from the GM products we are selling or developing. There have been numerous national and international scientific organizations that have reached this same conclusion, including the American Medical Association, the National Academy of Sciences, the World Health Organization and many others.

The year 2005 marked the tenth anniversary of large-scale cultivation of biotech crops, with more than a billion cumulative acres of production. Twenty-one countries–including Spain, Germany, Portugal, France and the Czech Republic–are commercially growing biotech crops. Benefits have been well documented, and measurable risks have not been found. Given limited farmland and the need to protect natural lands, it is critically important to increase food productivity on a per-acre basis, through advanced breeding and biotechnology.

The first generation of biotech crops has provided significant economic, environmental and grower benefits, and the next generation of biotech crops will provide much broader benefits. Some of these products include crops with improved tolerance to drought, more effective utilization of nitrogen, increased yield and enhanced nutrition.

We at Monsanto have pledged to listen better to and engage in dialogue with concerned groups, to be more transparent in the methods we use and the data we have about safety, to respect the cultural and ethical concerns of others, to share our technology with developing countries, and to make sure we deliver real benefits to our customers and to the environment. I think this new attitude and new set of commitments will help improve both our company's image and the acceptance of this new technology.

No – *Margaret Mellon, director of the food and environment program of the Union of Concerned Scientists in Washington, D.C., holds a law degree and a Ph.D. in molecular biology. She explains her concerns about the effects of GM foods on human health and the environment.*

Q: How did you become interested in genetically modified foods?

A: I became aware of genetic engineering while running a program on toxic chemicals at the Environmental Law Institute in the 1980s. I was initially more positively disposed toward biotechnology than I came to be over the years. Like a lot of folks, I wasn't very critical. But the more I knew about the technology and the deeper the questions I asked about it, the less likely I was to accept at face value the extravagant promises made on its behalf.

I should also say, however, that my colleagues and I at the Union of Concerned Scientists are not opposed to biotechnology. We think its use in research and drug manufacture, for example, is essential. The therapeutic benefits of the new drugs outweigh the risks, and often there aren't any alternatives. But in agriculture, it's different. So far, at least, there are only modest benefits associated with biotechnology products, and it has yet to be shown that the benefits outweigh the risks. And there are exciting alternatives to solving agricultural problems that we are simply ignoring.

Agriculture isn't like medicine. We in the U.S. produce far more food than we need. And we are so wealthy that whatever we can't produce we can buy from somebody else. As a result, there are about 300,000 food products on our grocery shelves and 10,000 new ones added every year. The notion that consumers in the U.S. fundamentally need new biotechnology foods isn't persuasive.

Q: But of course, many scientists and policy experts argue that *we do* need biotechnology to feed the world, especially people in the developing world.

A: That is an important question to ask because so many people–more than 800 million–are undernourished or hungry. But is genetic engineering the best or only solution? We have sufficient food now, but it doesn't get to those who need it. Most hungry people simply can't afford to buy what's already out there even when commodity prices are at all-time lows. How does genetic engineering address the problem of income disparity?

The real tragedy is that the debate about biotechnology is diverting attention from solving the problem of world hunger. I'd like to see people seriously asking the question, "What can we do to help the world's hungry feed themselves?" and then make a list of answers. Better technology, including genetic engineering, would be somewhere on the list, but it would not be at the top. Trade policy, infrastructure and land reform are much more important, yet they are barely mentioned.

Genetic engineering has a place and should not be taken off the table, but I don't believe it is a panacea for world hunger. Treating it as if it is distorts this important debate. It is also amazing to me how quickly some have dismissed the virtues of traditional breeding–the technology that, after all, made the U.S. into an agricultural powerhouse.

Q: Can we turn to another potential benefit that people claim for GM foods: agriculture that is more environmentally friendly?

A: Let's ask a question: What is a green agriculture? Is it one that doesn't depend on pesticides? I think it's a lot more than that, actually. But if we just consider avoiding pesticide use, we now have some data on the impacts of engineered crops. Surveys of American farmers by the Department of Agriculture show that the use of Bt [pest-resistant] corn aimed at the corn borer, for example, hasn't done much to reduce the application of pesticides to corn, because the vast majority of corn acreage isn't treated with pesticide to control that pest.

The introduction of Bt cotton, however, has resulted in a measurable drop in pesticide use. That's good for the environment and good for the farmers who cut their input costs. But this benefit will last only as long as the Bt trait keeps working. I think most scientists expect that the way Bt crops are being deployed will eventually lead to the evolution of resistance in the target pests, which means that the Bt cotton won't work anymore. We are likely to run through Bt cotton just like we ran through all the pesticides before it. So it isn't a durable path to a greener agriculture.

And there are environmental risks out there. Most scientists agree now that gene flow will occur–genes *will* go from engineered crops to nearby relatives. That means pollen will carry novel genes from the agricultural settings into neighbors' fields or into the wild. Widespread use of GM crops has already led to the creation of herbicide-resistant weeds in Canada and the U.S.

Q: What about the health risks of GM foods? Do you see any looming problems?

A: I know of no reason to say the foods currently on the market are not safe to consume. But I don't have as much confidence as I should in that statement. There was a letter published in the journal *Science* a few years ago from someone who had searched the literature for peer-reviewed studies comparing GM food to non-GM food. The researcher found something like five studies, a situation that persists to this day. That's not enough of a basis, from a scientific standpoint, to assure ourselves that these foods are safe.

I would say the biggest concern is the possibility of converting nonallergenic foods into allergens. Introducing new toxins into food is also a risk. Of course, breeders are going to try to avoid doing that, but plants have lots of toxins in them; as scientists manipulate systems that they don't completely understand, one of the unexpected effects could be turning on genes for toxins. There are rules that govern how genes come together and come apart in traditional breeding. We're not obeying those rules.

Q: So you don't see genetic engineering of crops to be an extension of traditional breeding?

A: No, not at all. You just can't get an elephant to mate with a corn plant. Scientists are making combinations of genes that are not found in nature.

From a scientific standpoint, there is no dispute that this is fundamentally different from what has been done before. And that it is unnatural. Now, because it's new and unnatural doesn't *necessarily* mean that it will prove to be more risky. But it is certainly a big enough break with what we have done before to demand an extra measure of caution.

And caution is particularly appropriate where the technology involves our food supply. Lots and lots of people—virtually the whole population—could be exposed to genetically engineered foods, and yet we have only a handful of studies in the peer-reviewed literature addressing their safety. The question is, Do we *assume* the technology is safe based on an argument that it's just a minor extension of traditional breeding, or do we *prove* it? The scientist in me wants to prove it's safe. Why rest on assumptions when you can go into the lab?

Q: Science can never prove that any technology is 100 percent safe. Will you ever be satisfied that we've tested GM foods enough? And how much risk is acceptable?

A: Sure, I could be satisfied that GM foods have been adequately tested. But it's premature to address that question now. Nobody is saying, "Look, we've got this large body of peer-reviewed experimental data comparing GM with non-GM foods on a number of criteria that demonstrate the food is safe."

When we have generated such a body of evidence, *then* there will be an issue of whether what we have is enough. And eventually, if things go well, we'll get to a point where we say, "We've been cautious, but now we're going to move ahead." But we're nowhere near that point now.

Obviously, we take risks all the time. But why are we taking these risks? If we didn't have an abundant food supply, if we didn't have something like 300,000 food products on our shelves already, then we would have an argument for taking this society-wide risk. But we've got plenty of food. In fact, we've got too much. And although we have many problems associated with our food system, they are not going to be solved by biotechnology.

The Truth about Genetically Modified Food

By David H. Freedman

Robert Goldberg sags into his desk chair and gestures at the air. "Frankenstein monsters, things crawling out of the lab," he says. "This the most depressing thing I've ever dealt with."

Goldberg, a plant molecular biologist at the University of California, Los Angeles, is not battling psychosis. He is expressing despair at the relentless need to confront what he sees as bogus fears over the health risks of genetically modified (GM) crops. Particularly frustrating to him, he says, is that this debate should have ended decades ago, when researchers produced a stream of exonerating evidence: "Today we're facing the same objections we faced 40 years ago."

Across campus, David Williams, a cellular biologist who specializes in vision, has the opposite complaint. "A lot of naive science has been involved in pushing this technology," he says. "Thirty years ago we didn't know that when you throw any gene into a different genome, the genome reacts to it. But now anyone in this field knows the genome is not a static environment. Inserted genes can be transformed by several different means, and it can happen generations later." The result, he insists, could very well be potentially toxic plants slipping through testing.

Williams concedes that he is among a tiny minority of biologists raising sharp questions about the safety of GM crops. But he says this is only because the field of plant molecular biology is protecting its interests. Funding, much of it from the companies that sell GM seeds, heavily favors researchers who are exploring ways to further the use of genetic modification in agriculture. He says that biologists who point out health or other risks associated with GM crops—who merely report or defend experimental findings that imply there may be risks—find themselves the focus of vicious attacks on their credibility, which leads scientists who see problems with GM foods to keep quiet.

Whether Williams is right or wrong, one thing is undeniable: despite overwhelming evidence that GM crops are safe to eat, the debate over their use continues to rage, and in some parts of the world, it is growing ever louder. Skeptics would argue that this contentiousness is a good thing–that we cannot be too cautious when tinkering with the genetic basis of the world's food supply. To researchers such as Goldberg, however, the persistence of fears about GM foods is nothing short of exasperating. "In spite of hundreds of millions of genetic experiments involving every type of organism on earth," he says, "and people eating billions of meals without a problem, we've gone back to being ignorant."

So who is right: advocates of GM or critics? When we look carefully at the evidence for both sides and weigh the risks and benefits, we find a surprisingly clear path out of this dilemma.

Benefits and Worries

The bulk of the science on GM safety points in one direction. Take it from David Zilberman, a U.C. Berkeley agricultural and environmental economist and one of the few researchers considered credible by both agricultural chemical companies and their critics. He argues that the benefits of GM crops greatly outweigh the health risks, which so far remain theoretical. The use of GM crops "has lowered the price of food," Zilberman says. "It has increased farmer safety by allowing them to use less pesticide. It has raised the output of corn, cotton and soy by 20 to 30 percent, allowing some people to survive who would not have without it. If it were more widely adopted around the world, the price [of food] would go lower, and fewer people would die of hunger."

In the future, Zilberman says, those advantages will become all the more significant. The United Nations Food and Agriculture Organization estimates that the world will have to grow 70 percent more food by 2050 just to keep up with population growth. Climate change will make much of the world's arable land more difficult to farm. GM crops, Zilberman says, could produce higher yields, grow in dry and salty land, withstand high and low temperatures, and tolerate insects, disease and herbicides.

Despite such promise, much of the world has been busy banning, restricting and otherwise shunning GM foods. Nearly all the corn and soybeans grown in the U.S. are genetically modified, but only two GM crops, Monsanto's MON810 maize and BASF's Amflora potato, are accepted in the European Union. Ten E.U. nations have banned MON810, and although BASF withdrew Amflora from the market in 2012, four E.U. nations have taken the trouble to ban that, too. Approval of a few new GM corn strains has been proposed there, but so far it has been repeatedly and soundly voted down. Throughout Asia, including in India and China, governments have yet to approve most GM crops, including an insect-resistant rice that produces higher yields with less pesticide. In Africa, where millions go hungry, several nations have refused to import GM foods in spite of their lower costs (the result of higher yields and a reduced need for water and pesticides). Kenya has banned them altogether amid widespread malnutrition. No country has definite plans to grow Golden Rice, a crop engineered to deliver more vitamin A than spinach (rice normally has no vitamin A), even though vitamin A deficiency causes more than one million deaths annually and half a million cases of irreversible blindness in the developing world.

Globally, only a tenth of the world's cropland includes GM plants. Four countries–the U.S., Canada, Brazil and Argentina–grow 90 percent of the planet's GM crops. Other Latin American countries are pushing away from the plants. And even in the U.S., voices decrying genetically modified foods are becoming louder. In 2016 the U.S. federal government passed a law requiring labeling of GM ingredients in food products, replacing GM-labeling laws in force or proposed in several dozen states.

The fear fueling all this activity has a long history. The public has been worried about the safety of GM foods since scientists at the University of Washington developed the first genetically

BASICS

How to Build a Better Plant

Genetic modification and conventional plant breeding have much in common: both are ways of producing new crops by altering plant genomes. The differences have to do with the tools used, the number of genes swapped and the comfort level of the average consumer.

Conventional Crossbreeding

Since the earliest days of agriculture, humans have been selecting plants with desirable characteristics and crossbreeding them to make new, even more desirable specimens—in this case, a tomato plant that combines the blight resistance of one parent with the high fruit yield of another.

Genetic Modification

In the 1970s scientists began developing methods for quickly inserting specific genes from one plant into the DNA of another—a quick, targeted means to the same end as conventional crossbreeding. Early researchers used disarmed *Agrobacterium* to smuggle genes into plant cells. Later, scientists at Cornell University developed the DNA particle gun method, in which engineers shoot DNA-coated tungsten balls through the cell walls of the target plant by firing them out of a blank gunpowder cartridge.

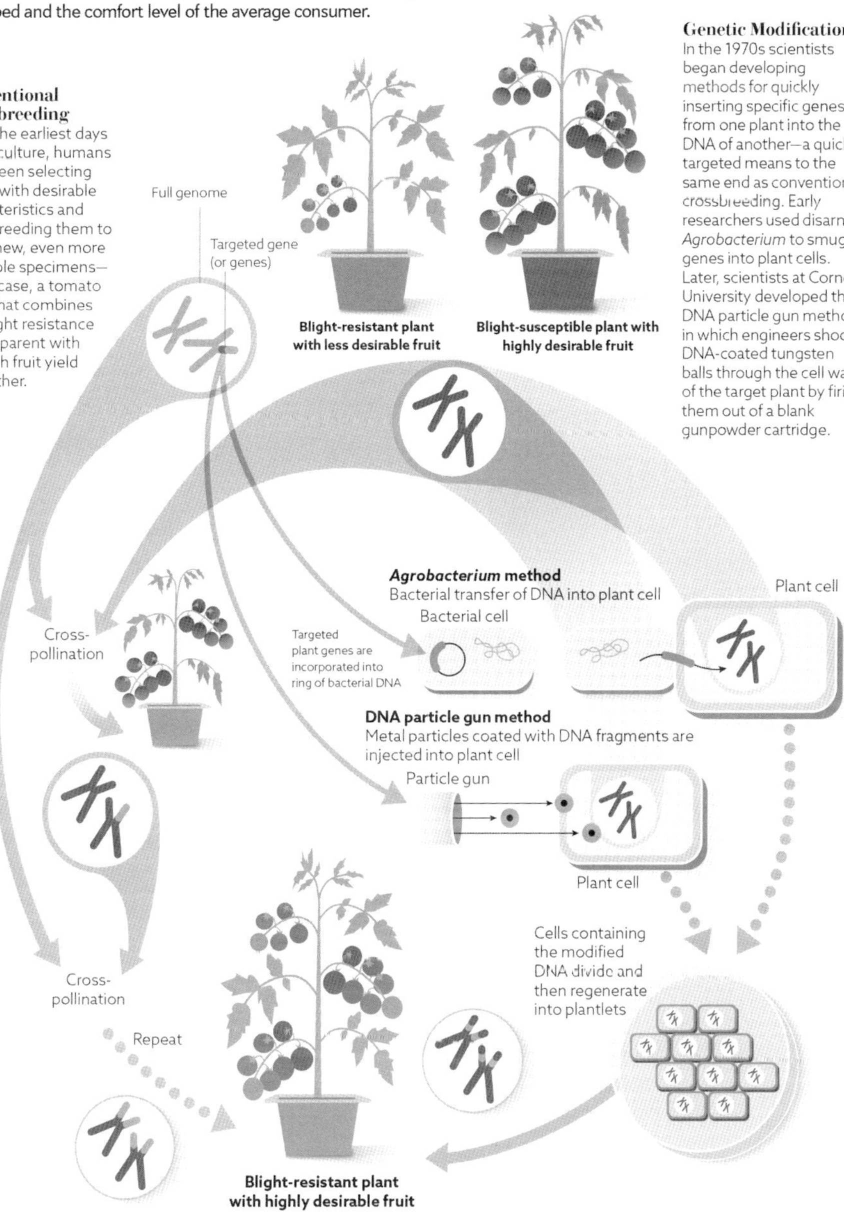

Credit: Jen Christiansen

modified tobacco plants in the 1970s. In the mid-1990s, when the first GM crops reached the market, Greenpeace, the Sierra Club, Ralph Nader, Prince Charles and a number of celebrity chefs took highly visible stands against them. Consumers in Europe became particularly alarmed: a survey conducted in 1997, for example, found that 69 percent of the Austrian public saw serious risks in GM foods, compared with only 14 percent of Americans.

In Europe, skepticism about GM foods has long been bundled with other concerns, such as a resentment of American agribusiness. Whatever it is based on, however, the European attitude reverberates across the world, influencing policy in countries where GM crops could have tremendous benefits. "In Africa, they don't care what us savages in America are doing," Zilberman says. "They look to Europe and see countries there rejecting GM, so they don't use it." Forces fighting genetic modification in Europe have rallied support for "the precautionary principle," which holds that given the kind of catastrophe that would emerge from loosing a toxic, invasive GM crop on the world, GM efforts should be shut down until the technology is proved absolutely safe.

But as medical researchers know, nothing can really be "proved safe." One can only fail to turn up significant risk after trying hard to find it—as is the case with GM crops.

A Clean Record

The human race has been selectively breeding crops, thus altering plants' genomes, for millennia. Ordinary wheat has long been strictly a human-engineered plant; it could not exist outside of farms, because its seeds do not scatter. For some 60 years scientists have been using "mutagenic" techniques to scramble the DNA of plants with radiation and chemicals, creating strains of wheat, rice, peanuts and pears that have become agricultural mainstays. The practice has inspired little objection from scientists or the public and has caused no known health problems.

The difference is that selective breeding or mutagenic techniques tend to result in large swaths of genes being swapped or altered. GM technology, in contrast, enables scientists to insert into a plant's genome a single gene (or a few of them) from another species of plant or even from a bacterium, virus or animal. Supporters argue that this precision makes the technology much less likely to produce surprises. Most plant molecular biologists also say that in the highly unlikely case that an unexpected health threat emerged from a new GM plant, scientists would quickly identify and eliminate it. "We know where the gene goes and can measure the activity of every single gene around it," Goldberg says. "We can show exactly which changes occur and which don't."

And although it might seem creepy to add virus DNA to a plant, doing so is, in fact, no big deal, proponents say. Viruses have been inserting their DNA into the genomes of crops, as well as humans and all other organisms, for millions of years. They often deliver the genes of other species while they are at it, which is why our own genome is loaded with genetic sequences that originated in viruses and nonhuman species. "When GM critics say that genes don't cross the species barrier in nature, that's just simple ignorance," says Alan McHughen, a plant molecular geneticist at U.C. Riverside. Pea aphids contain fungi genes. Triticale is a century-plus-old hybrid of wheat and rye found in some flours and breakfast cereals. Wheat itself, for that matter, is a cross-species hybrid. "Mother Nature does it all the time, and so do conventional plant breeders," McHughen says.

Could eating plants with altered genes allow new DNA to work its way into our own? It is possible but hugely improbable. Scientists have never found genetic material that could survive a trip through the human gut and make it into cells. Besides, we are routinely exposed to—and even consume—the viruses and bacteria whose genes end up in GM foods. The bacterium *Bacillus thuringiensis*, for example, which produces proteins fatal to insects, is sometimes enlisted as a natural pesticide in organic farming. "We've been eating this stuff for thousands of years," Goldberg says.

In any case, proponents say, people have consumed as many as trillions of meals containing genetically modified ingredients over the past few decades. Not a single verified case of illness has ever been attributed to the genetic alterations. Mark Lynas, a prominent anti-GM activist who in 2013 publicly switched to strongly supporting the technology, has pointed out that every single news-making food disaster on record has been attributed to non-GM crops, such as the *Escherichia coli*–infected organic bean sprouts that killed 53 people in Europe in 2011.

Critics often disparage U.S. research on the safety of genetically modified foods, which is often funded or even conducted by GM companies, such as Monsanto. But much research on the subject comes from the European Commission, the administrative body of the E.U., which cannot be so easily dismissed as an industry tool. The European Commission has funded 130 research projects, carried out by more than 500 independent teams, on the safety of GM crops. None of those studies found any special risks from GM crops.

Plenty of other credible groups have arrived at the same conclusion. Gregory Jaffe, director of biotechnology at the Center for Science in the Public Interest, a science-based consumer-watchdog group in Washington, D.C., takes pains to note that the center has no official stance, pro or con, with regard to genetically modifying food plants. Yet Jaffe insists the scientific record is clear. "Current GM crops are safe to eat and can be grown safely in the environment," he says. The American Association for the Advancement of Science, the American Medical Association and the National Academy of Sciences have all unreservedly backed GM crops. The U.S. Food and Drug Administration, along with its counterparts in several other countries, has repeatedly reviewed large bodies of research and concluded that GM crops pose no unique health threats. Dozens of review studies carried out by academic researchers have backed that view.

Opponents of genetically modified foods point to a handful of studies indicating possible safety problems. But reviewers have dismantled almost all of those reports. For example, a 1998 study by plant biochemist Árpád Pusztai, then at the Rowett Institute in Scotland, found that rats fed a GM potato suffered from stunted growth and immune system–related changes. But the potato was not intended for human consumption–it was, in fact, designed to be toxic for research purposes. The Rowett Institute later deemed the experiment so sloppy that it refuted the findings and charged Pusztai with misconduct.

Similar stories abound. Most recently, a team led by Gilles-Éric Séralini, a researcher at the University of Caen Lower Normandy in France, found that rats eating a common type of GM corn contracted cancer at an alarmingly high rate. But Séralini has long been an anti-GM campaigner, and critics charged that in his study, he relied on a strain of rat that too easily develops tumors, did not use enough rats, did not include proper control groups and failed to report many details of the experiment, including how the analysis was performed. After a review, the European Food Safety Authority dismissed the study's findings. Several other European agencies came to the same conclusion. "If GM corn were that toxic, someone would have noticed by now," McHughen says. "Séralini has been refuted by everyone who has cared to comment."

Some scientists say the objections to GM food stem from politics rather than science–that they are motivated by an objection to large multinational corporations having enormous influence over the food supply; invoking risks from genetic modification just provides a convenient way of whipping up the masses against industrial agriculture. "This has nothing to do with science," Goldberg says. "It's about ideology." Former anti-GM activist Lynas agrees. He has gone as far as labeling the anti-GM crowd "explicitly an antiscience movement."

Persistent Doubts

Not all objections to genetically modified foods are so easily dismissed, however. Long-term health effects can be subtle and nearly impossible to link to specific changes in the environment.

Scientists have long believed that Alzheimer's disease and many cancers have environmental components, but few would argue we have identified all of them.

And opponents say that it is not true that the GM process is less likely to cause problems simply because fewer, more clearly identified genes are replaced. David Schubert, an Alzheimer's researcher who heads the Cellular Neurobiology Laboratory at the Salk Institute for Biological Studies in La Jolla, Calif., asserts that a single, well-characterized gene can still settle in the target plant's genome in many different ways. "It can go in forward, backward, at different locations, in multiple copies, and they all do different things," he says. And as U.C.L.A.'s Williams notes, a genome often continues to change in the successive generations after the insertion, leaving it with a different arrangement than the one intended and initially tested. There is also the phenomenon of "insertional mutagenesis," Williams adds, in which the insertion of a gene ends up quieting the activity of nearby genes.

True, the number of genes affected in a GM plant most likely will be far, far smaller than in conventional breeding techniques. Yet opponents maintain that because the wholesale swapping or alteration of entire packages of genes is a natural process that has been happening in plants for half a billion years, it tends to produce few scary surprises today. Changing a single gene, on the other hand, might turn out to be a more subversive action, with unexpected ripple effects, including the production of new proteins that might be toxins or allergens.

Opponents also point out that the kinds of alterations caused by the insertion of genes from other species might be more impactful, more complex or more subtle than those caused by the intraspecies gene swapping of conventional breeding. And just because there is no evidence to date that genetic material from an altered crop can make it into the genome of people who eat it does not mean such a transfer will never happen—or that it has not already happened and we have yet to spot it. These changes might be difficult to catch; their impact on the production of proteins might not even turn up in testing. "You'd certainly find out if the result is that the plant doesn't grow very well," Williams says. "But will you find the change if it results in the production of proteins with long-term effects on the health of the people eating it?"

It is also true that many pro-GM scientists in the field are unduly harsh—even unscientific—in their treatment of critics. GM proponents sometimes lump every scientist who raises safety questions together with activists and discredited researchers. And even Séralini, the scientist behind the study that found high cancer rates for GM-fed rats, has his defenders. Most of them are nonscientists, or retired researchers from obscure institutions, or nonbiologist scientists, but the Salk Institute's Schubert also insists the study was unfairly dismissed. He says that as someone who runs drug-safety studies, he is well versed on what constitutes a good-quality animal toxicology study and that Séralini's makes the grade. He insists that the breed of rat in the study is commonly used in respected drug studies, typically in numbers no greater than in Séralini's study; that the methodology was standard; and that the details of the data analysis are irrelevant because the results were so striking.

Schubert joins Williams as one of a handful of biologists from respected institutions who are willing to sharply challenge the GM-foods-are-safe majority. Both charge that more scientists would speak up against genetic modification if doing so did not invariably lead to being excoriated in journals and the media. These attacks, they argue, are motivated by the fear that airing doubts could lead to less funding for the field. Says Williams: "Whether it's conscious or not, it's in their interest to promote this field, and they're not objective."

Both scientists say that after publishing comments in respected journals questioning the safety of GM foods, they became the victims of coordinated attacks on their reputations. Schubert even charges that researchers who turn up results that might raise safety questions avoid publishing their findings out of fear of repercussions. "If it doesn't come out the right way," he says, "you're going to get trashed."

There is evidence to support that charge. In 2009 *Nature* detailed the backlash to a reasonably solid study published in the *Proceedings of the National Academy of Sciences USA* by researchers from Loyola University Chicago and the University of Notre Dame. The paper showed that GM corn seemed to be finding its way from farms into nearby streams and that it might pose a risk to some insects there because, according to the researchers' lab studies, caddis flies appeared to suffer on diets of pollen from GM corn. Many scientists immediately attacked the study, some of them suggesting the researchers were sloppy to the point of misconduct.

A Way Forward

There is a middle ground in this debate. Many moderate voices call for continuing the distribution of GM foods while maintaining or even stepping up safety testing on new GM crops. They advocate keeping a close eye on the health and environmental impact of existing ones. But they do not single out GM crops for special scrutiny, the Center for Science in the Public Interest's Jaffe notes: *all* crops could use more testing. "We should be doing a better job with food oversight altogether," he says.

Even Schubert agrees. In spite of his concerns, he believes future GM crops can be introduced safely if testing is improved. "Ninety percent of the scientists I talk to assume that new GM plants are safety-tested the same way new drugs are by the FDA," he says. "They absolutely aren't, and they absolutely should be."

Stepped-up testing would pose a burden for GM researchers, and it could slow down the introduction of new crops. "Even under the current testing standards for GM crops, most conventionally bred crops wouldn't have made it to market," McHughen says. "What's going to happen if we become even more strict?"

That is a fair question. But with governments and consumers increasingly coming down against GM crops altogether, additional testing may be the compromise that enables the human race to benefit from those crops' significant advantages.

Referenced

Food, Inc.: Mendel to Monsanto—The Promises and Perils of the Biotech Harvest. Peter Pringle. Simon & Schuster, 2003.

Tough Lessons from Golden Rice. Martin Enserink in *Science*, Vol. 320, pages 468–471; April 25, 2008.

Case Studies: A Hard Look at GM Crops. Natasha Gilbert in *Nature*, Vol. 497, pages 24–26; May 2, 2013. www.nature.com/news/case-studies-a-hard-look-at-gm-crops-1.12907

About the Author

David H. Freedman is a journalist who has been covering science, business and technology for more than 30 years.

Do Seed Companies Control GM Crop Research?

By The Editors

Advances in agricultural technology—including, but not limited to, the genetic modification of food crops—have made fields more productive than ever. Farmers grow more crops and feed more people using less land. They are able to use fewer pesticides and to reduce the amount of tilling that leads to erosion. And within the next two years, agritech companies plan to introduce advanced crops that are designed to survive heat waves and droughts, resilient characteristics that will become increasingly important in a world marked by a changing climate. Unfortunately, it is impossible to verify that genetically modified crops perform as advertised. That is because agritech companies have given themselves veto power over the work of independent researchers.

To purchase genetically modified seeds, a customer must sign an agreement that limits what can be done with them. (If you have installed software recently, you will recognize the concept of the end-user agreement.) Agreements are considered necessary to protect a company's intellectual property, and they justifiably preclude the replication of the genetic enhancements that make the seeds unique. But agritech companies such as Monsanto, Pioneer and Syngenta go further. For a decade their user agreements have explicitly forbidden the use of the seeds for any independent research. Under the threat of litigation, scientists cannot test a seed to explore the different conditions under which it thrives or fails. They cannot compare seeds from one company against those from another company. And perhaps most important, they cannot examine whether the genetically modified crops lead to unintended environmental side effects.

Research on genetically modified seeds is still published, of course. But only studies that the seed companies have approved ever see the light of a peer-reviewed journal. In a number of cases, experiments that had the implicit go-ahead from the seed company were later blocked from publication because the results were not flattering. "It is important to understand that it is not always simply a matter of blanket denial of all research requests, which is bad enough," wrote Elson J. Shields, an entomologist at Cornell University, in a letter to an official at the Environmental Protection Agency (the body tasked with regulating the environmental consequences of genetically modified crops), "but selective denials and permissions based on industry perceptions of how 'friendly' or 'hostile' a particular scientist may be toward [seed-enhancement] technology."

Shields is the spokesperson for a group of 24 corn insect scientists that opposes these practices. Because the scientists rely on the cooperation of the companies for their research–they must, after all, gain access to the seeds for studies–most have chosen to remain anonymous for fear of reprisals. The group has submitted a statement to the EPA protesting that "as a result of restricted access, no truly independent research can be legally conducted on many critical questions regarding the technology."

It would be chilling enough if any other type of company were able to prevent independent researchers from testing its wares and reporting what they find–imagine car companies trying to quash head-to-head model comparisons done by *Consumer Reports*, for example. But when scientists are prevented from examining the raw ingredients in our nation's food supply or from testing the plant material that covers a large portion of the country's agricultural land, the restrictions on free inquiry become dangerous.

Although we appreciate the need to protect the intellectual property rights that have spurred the investments into research and development that have led to agritech's successes, we also believe food safety and environmental protection depend on making plant products available to regular scientific scrutiny. Agricultural technology companies should therefore immediately remove the restriction on research from their end-user agreements. Going forward, the EPA should also require, as a condition of approving the sale of new seeds, that independent researchers have unfettered access to all products currently on the market. The agricultural revolution is too important to keep locked behind closed doors.

How Biotech Crops Can Crash—and Still Never Fail

By Aniket Aga and Maywa Montenegro de Wit

The United Nations Food Systems Summit held last September was eclipsed by a powerful countermobilization effort led by farmers and scientists, as well as civil society groups allied with Indigenous communities and small-scale food producers across the world. These are the very people critical to achieving the summit's stated goals of ending hunger and promoting sustainable agriculture. The scientists and advocates accused summit organizers of compromising on food security, democratic accountability, sustainability, and the human rights of producers and workers in favor of transnational agribusinesses.

Opposition to the summit had been mounting since July, when hundreds of grassroots organizations challenged the organizers for framing the problem of food systems in narrow, technocratic ways and offering "false solutions" such as biotechnological interventions instead of promoting more sustainable, just and people-first ways of farming. Also in July the Philippines approved commercial cultivation of Bt eggplant, a genetically modified (GM) food that produces a protein that kills eggplant fruit and shoot borers, and "Golden Rice" altered to produce beta-carotene, the precursor of vitamin A. The Philippines thus became the first country in South and Southeast Asia to approve GM rice and the second in the world after Bangladesh to approve GM eggplant.

Advocates of GM crops hailed the Philippines' move as a triumph of science. Since the U.N.'s food summit was announced two years ago, different groups have steadily reduced applications of science to global problems to a limited set of investor-oriented innovations. Within this orbit, agricultural biotechnology and digitalization are touted as vital to achieving the U.N.'s sustainable development goals.

As governments now debate the way forward from the summit, it is critical to recognize that a narrow focus on technology to address the complex structural problems of farming and food has an astonishingly poor track record. In more than two decades of GM crops' cultivation, nearly every aspect of GM crop research, development and application has stoked scientific controversy.

At its base, GM crops are rooted in a colonial-capitalist model of agriculture based on theft of Indigenous land and on exploiting farmers' and food workers' labor, women's bodies, Indigenous knowledge and the web of life itself. The green revolution of the 1960s exported this paradigm to ex-colonial countries in South and Southeast Asia. Today this agricultural model is responsible not only for soaring farm debt, depleted soils, and threats to native seeds and biodiversity but also the erosion of farmers' knowledge and skills. The same model stands implicated in the emergence of novel pathogens and our increased vulnerability to pandemics. For the world to achieve sustainability, this colonial model of agriculture must be dismantled, and promising agroecological approaches premised on working with biodiversity and farmers' knowledge and skills should be brought center stage.

Maize and soy, along with cotton and canola, dominate the GM market. Most GM crops are engineered with resistance to herbicides and insects, which has not only contributed to the emergence of "superweeds" and soaring pesticide use but has driven the global consolidation of seed and chemical industries. These kinds of crops have principally benefited large-scale farmers, grain traders and multinational behemoths involved in selling seeds and pesticides.

Despite these problems, multinational agribusinesses have latched onto Golden Rice and Bt eggplant as ostensibly pro-poor technologies to win over smallholder farmers and consumers in the Global South. Since 2008 the International Rice Research Institute, based in the Philippines, has led Golden Rice's development with support from the Bill & Melinda Gates Foundation and in partnership with Syngenta (which owns rights to the rice) to address vitamin A deficiency (VAD) among the poor, especially children and pregnant women.

A crucial, unresolved question has been whether children can actually absorb beta-carotene from the rice. Its vitamin A content is low—relative to other, culturally more appropriate sources such as carrots and some leafy vegetables—and degrades with storage at room temperature, exposure to air and cooking.

The only available feeding study, published in 2009, had adult subjects eating Golden Rice, along with butter, oil, cashew nuts, meat and salad. More than 300 kilocalories came from fats, which aid the absorption of vitamin A. These conditions are hardly representative of poor, food-insecure households. Further, while efforts to introduce the trait into a local rice in Bangladesh have met with some success, in India, similar efforts resulted in a variety unsuitable for cultivation.

Such serious limitations would have derailed another project but not Golden Rice. In an exercise in grandstanding, more than 120 Nobel laureates endorsed an emotive appeal in 2016 supporting Golden Rice. This campaign involved figures such as a former Monsanto PR executive. Meanwhile studies by the Food and Nutrition Research Institute indicate marked success in combating vitamin A deficiency *without* any Golden Rice. Nutrition education, capsule supplements and other public programs in the Philippines have brought VAD down from a peak of 40.1 percent in 2003 to 15.5 percent in 2018–2019.

Bt eggplant was developed by the Indian company Mahyco, in which Monsanto held a 26 percent stake. It has stalled in India for more than a decade in part because of serious concerns of inducing antibiotic resistance in consumers, critically flawed toxicological analyses and threats to biodiversity. The same GMO has, however, been successfully marketed in Bangladesh and now the Philippines by actors linked to the Cornell Alliance for Science (a group backed by the Gates Foundation) and USAID. It is showcased as an innovation that will reduce both pesticide usage and losses from the eggplant fruit and shoot borer.

Yet research to support these claims tends to be both short-term and limited largely to monetary parameters. Bt cotton in India was marketed, starting in 2002, on the same twin planks of reduction in pesticide usage and losses from bollworms. Reviewing 18 years of experience, scientists found that pink bollworms became resistant to Bt cotton within a few years of large-scale adoption, forcing farmers to spray lethal amounts and fatal combinations of pesticides. The review concluded that Bt cotton's primary contribution to Indian agriculture was escalating pesticide use and costs of cultivation "rather than any enduring agronomic benefits."

GM crops have already saturated markets in corn, canola and soy in North and South America. For expansion, agribusiness is eyeing markets in lower-income countries and looking at smallholder crops, such as eggplant, millet and cassava. It is also assessing the use of gene editing as a tool to modify crop genomes.

It is therefore no surprise that the special envoy to the U.N. Food Systems Summit, Agnes Kalibata, was chosen from the Gates Foundation–sponsored Alliance for a Green Revolution in Africa. Nor is it surprising that after the U.N. entered into a strategic partnership with the World Economic Forum, summit science has come to mirror the forum's "fourth industrial revolution" approach to food systems change.

To connect investor-friendly tech innovations to the WEF's plank of free trade, the summit's leadership presents a simplistic picture of science–where technology innovates food systems without considerations of power and politics.

Yet decades of research has shown how biotechnology science is path-dependent, becoming more powerful as things such as patents make it increasingly lucrative for universities to do biotech research. More biotech research means more lab facilities, faculty and staff jobs, along with greater funding to support students who pursue this line of work. Over time, it has progressively become harder to conduct and publish research critical of GM crops. In effect, biotechnology has "locked out" other innovations, including agroecology.

Still, the case for agroecology grows stronger the more researchers learn. For instance, in 2009 a study comparing 840 MASIPAG farmers, part of a farmer-scientist network in the Philippines, found that 88 percent of agroecological adopters saw improvements in their food security, compared with 44 percent of nonadopters. Farmers who transitioned to agroecology ate 68 percent more vegetables, 56 percent more fruit, 55 percent more protein-rich staples and 40 percent more meat than before. New research by Debal Deb of the Center for Interdisciplinary Studies in India shows that mixed cropping patterns of Indigenous farmers in eastern India are significantly more productive than the single-cropping model of industrial farming.

Critics like to say these studies are cherry-picked. But the High Level Panel of Experts in 2019 took this challenge on. Its results show that agroecology has received much less investment in R&D than ecofriendly spins on the dominant technocratic approaches. Yet agroecology continues to generate ecological and social gains across scales, particularly when formal research institutions recognize the expertise of social movements and when women's rights are central. Biodiversity-rich farms with complex relationships among multiple species are also more resilient and sustainable. A new meta-analysis of two decades of research found that agroecological practices improve nutrition and food security outcomes in low- and middle-income countries–and the more practices farmers included, the greater the benefits.

To say that smallholder and Indigenous agroecologists are experts in their own right is not to say things are fine for them. COVID-19 brought preexisting vulnerabilities and inequalities into sharp relief. It highlighted that a food system based on global supply chains, market-led food provision and export orientation–exactly the approach promoted by the U.N. Food Systems Summit–is brittle and prone to crisis. Rather than celebrate grossly inadequate and unscientific solutions, the global community must support what hundreds of millions of agriculturalists represented by the Civil Society and Indigenous Peoples' Mechanism are asking for: robust international support for agroecology within a governing framework of human rights, peasant rights, and food sovereignty.

About the Authors

Aniket Aga teaches environmental studies and anthropology at Krea University in India. He is the author of Genetically Modified Democracy: Transgenic Crops in Contemporary India*, published by Yale University Press.*

Maywa Montenegro de Wit is an assistant professor in the department of environmental studies at the University of California, Santa Cruz. Combining theories and methods from political ecology, science and technology studies, and agroecology, she studies knowledge politics in struggles for just and sustainable food systems.

Designer Crops of the Future Must Be Better Tailored for Women in Agriculture

By Vivian Polar and Matty Demont

For all the progress that scientists have made in breeding crops that feed more people, these breakthroughs typically elude a core demographic in low-income countries that rely on agriculture: women.

Advances in seed genetics are estimated to be responsible for up to 60 percent of yield increases in farmers' fields in recent years by making crops hardier and faster-maturing. However, only a third of crops grown by sub-Saharan African farmers in 2010 were the latest varieties of genetically improved plants; the uptake is as low as 5 percent for women-led households in that region. In some cases, modern varieties may be more difficult for women to harvest, process or cook but ultimately, scientists need more research to fully understand the traits that make crops desirable and viable for women as well as men.

Women make up more than 40 percent of the global agricultural workforce, and an even greater proportion in developing countries. In order to improve global food security and end hunger, crop breeders need better market intelligence to understand the qualities women prefer in crops so they, too, can access the gains from genetically engineered crops.

Whereas men who farm are more likely to prioritize high yields and disease resistance, since this typically equates to higher incomes upon selling, women who farm often prioritize other needs in their roles as mothers, caregivers and custodians of households. The implication for crop breeders is that for a new variety to be widely adopted by both men and women, it must be attractive both to men looking to increase earnings, and women, who take on a greater responsibility for household nutrition.

Scientists are starting to make headway in understanding the needs of women farmers. For instance, in a forthcoming study by the International Potato Center (CIP), researchers working on new varieties of sweet potato for East Africa found that 80 percent of stakeholders were aware that women prioritised the taste of sweet potato varieties over all other traits because this impacts the likelihood of their children eating it. Another example is demand for rice fragrance in South and Southeast Asia, which was found to be mainly driven by women.

This is reinforced by other studies that indicate that the ease of cooking for staple crops such as cassava is also a key factor that influences the uptake of new varieties among women. They tend to prefer varieties that cook quickly during boiling, which is determined by factors such as age, phytic acid levels and larger starch granules.

But as well as women's preferences, crop breeders also need more market intelligence to better understand the challenges and barriers to uptake that women face and their role in household decision-making on what crop varieties to grow. For example, research shows that women are more likely to take on the time-consuming manual work of weeding, threshing and cooking; weeding a single hectare of sorghum by hand takes up to 324 hours of labor. In East Africa, maize adoption lagged because women objected to higher-yield varieties of hard dent maize that were difficult to grind and so increased their workload. Women are more likely to use traits that reduce the drudgery of agriculture for them.

Early efforts to factor in these considerations in the crop breeding process have included the development of G+ Tools by CGIAR (formerly the Consultative Group on International Agricultural Research), the organization for which we work. It's the world's largest publicly funded agricultural organization. This tool kit provides a framework to support targeting specific segments of the population to determine the potential implications of traits or varieties for gender equality. The tools include questions about how a new product might increase drudgery, displace other forms of income or rely too heavily on inputs such as irrigation, mechanization or fertilizer, which may be out of reach for women.

The tools, which unite the expertise of social scientists, gender experts and breeders, have been piloted in Uganda, Nigeria and Zimbabwe to set priorities for the development of new lines of sweet potato, cassava and beans. In Nigeria, this has led to the cassava breeding program prioritizing traits that are important to women who process cassava-based foods, including sweetness, low fiber, low moisture levels, ease of peeling and the preferred color for consumers.

Breeders also need to go beyond the field to understand the needs of women in agribusiness at every stage of the value chain. With more investment into projects and initiatives that subsidize the rollout of new varieties, farmers and processors could afford to test them and see their benefits before adopting them in full, so as not to compromise their traditional sources of income and food.

And for all the crops that provide better yields for smallholders, those that perish quickly or that need specific storage conditions to reach market or specialist equipment to process will be less profitable and therefore less likely to be adopted.

Among the existing innovations that hold promise for better nutrition and livelihoods against the pressures of climate change are vitamin-enriched sweet potato and cassava, iron and zinc-biofortified and low glycemic index rice, high-yielding maize and fast-cooking beans. But fine-tuning these varieties to maximize their uptake among men and women needs more research into their needs on the ground.

An estimated $39 million investment is needed over the next three years to design these crops and tailor them, but the return is likely to translate to higher incomes, improved food security and greater levels of equality for up to 125 million farmers, small businesses, and consumers across Africa and South Asia alone by 2030. And by meeting the needs of all farmers, improved varieties can future-proof food systems for everyone.

This is an opinion and analysis article, and the views expressed by the author or authors are not necessarily those of Scientific American.

About the Authors

Vivian Polar is the gender and innovation senior specialist at the CGIAR International Potato Center (CIP) CGIAR (formerly the Consultative Group on International Agricultural Research).

Matty Demont is the research leader, markets, consumers and nutrition, at the CGIAR International Rice Research Institute (IRRI) of CGIAR (formerly the Consultative Group on International Agricultural Research).

Should the Concept of a Food Desert Be Deserted?

By Layla Eplett

Originally introduced by British politicians in the 1990s, the concept of a food desert has been a popular way to approach food insecure regions in the United States for over a decade. It has been embraced by politicians, celebrities, chefs, and other influential leaders. Despite this trend, the term "food desert" and efficacy of the interventions to combat them have been questioned in recent years.

"Most simply, people talk about food deserts as places where it is hard to access healthy and affordable food," says Richard Sadler, a public health professor at the Flint campus of Michigan State University. Sadler co-authored a paper with Jason Andrew Gilliland and Godwin Arku that explores the theoretical issues surrounding debates around food deserts.

As Sadler explains, it's the simplicity of the definition that makes it appealing to some and can lead to interventions that are straightforward, like placing a grocery store in an area that is deemed a food desert. He adds that this is what others are critical of–some contend that such a basic definition renders interventions to be one-dimensional and less effective.

Flint, Michigan may be known most for lead and other toxic contaminants in its water system, but the city also suffers from food insecurity and malnutrition. Another study by Sadler, Gilliland, and Arku examined the impact of a retail-based intervention in a socioeconomically disadvantaged area of Flint. Highlighting how malnutrition and food insecurity results from more than geographical access, their research found the introduction of a grocery store in the area did not have a significant impact on fruit and vegetable consumption. Further, there was an increase in the amount of prepared and fast foods consumed during the 17 months the grocery store was open.

Other studies have had similar findings regarding improvement in nutrition. The link between food deserts and obesity has been challenged and the need to consider cost and marketing has also been highlighted.

The use of the term "food desert" has been debated among scholars due to methodological issues and a lack of consensus over its definition. It has also been rejected due to its bleak imagery as well as its potential racial implications. Since the areas aren't completely absent of food, some believe a more accurate description would be to specify them as "fresh food deserts" or "health food deserts." Some suggest abandoning the use of "desert," and call them "junk food jungles" or "food swamps" instead. Sadler says he uses "food desert" cautiously, adding, "There is a part that we have to be critical of but I think it can still be a useful rhetorical device because there is a general understanding of what it means."

Beyond debates over semantics, Sadler thinks it is also important to consider how so-called food deserts are approached. Reflecting on health geography, researchers Robin Kearns and Graham Moon asked, "Is it more effective to do this through insurgency or collaboration?" Sadler sees this as a relevant question for approaches to food systems.

Following the closure of the Flint grocery store that was open for 17 months, another one has opened in its place. Sadler believes it may be having more success and partially attributes that to their community engagement–their existing presence at the local farmer's market and other factors has made them more attuned to their clients' needs. Other measures that actively collaborate with the community, like local food networks including community gardens, and non-commercialized food production have also had more positive outcomes.

Along with more in-depth discussions about the complexity of food deserts and a need to increase smaller scale collaborative interventions, Sadler says previous policies and projects should also be re-evaluated. "Now that we have this key information and continue learn more about what does and doesn't work, that should also shape the approach to food deserts."

The views expressed are those of the author(s) and are not necessarily those of Scientific American.

About the Author

Layla Eplett writes about the anthropology of food. She has a Masters in Social Anthropology of Development from the University of London's School of Oriental and African Studies and loves getting a taste of all kinds of culture—gastronomic, traditional, and sometimes accidentally, bacterial. Find her at Fare Trade.

Bill Gates Should Stop Telling Africans What Kind of Agriculture Africans Need

By Million Belay and Bridget Mugambe

Africans have long been told that our agriculture is backward and should be abandoned for a 21st-century version of the Green Revolution that enabled India to feed itself. Western science and technology, in the form of seeds modified by science and technology, synthetic fertilizers and pesticides, petroleum-fueled machinery and artificial irrigation were key to that miracle, we are informed, and we too need to tread that path.

A primary proponent of this view is the Cornell Alliance for Science (CAS), founded in 2014 to "depolarize the charged debate" around genetically modified (GM) seeds. With $22 million in funding thus far from the Bill and Melinda Gates Foundation, the CAS in fact consistently defends GM seeds, arguing that they are healthy, productive and environmentally friendly, while attacking agroecology as economically and socially regressive.

In contrast, the Alliance for Food Sovereignty in Africa (AFSA), which represents more than 200 million farmers, fishers, pastoralists, indigenous peoples, women, consumers and others across all but five African countries, holds that agroecology is what our continent needs. Small-scale, ecofriendly cultivation methods using indigenous knowledge and inputs and cutting-edge science increase the variety, nutritive value and quantity of foods produced on farms while stabilizing rural economies, promoting gender equity and protecting biodiversity.

This mission has put our alliance, the largest social movement in Africa, at odds with the CAS and by extension the Gates Foundation. And they are winning. On June 17, 2021, GRAIN, a small nonprofit organization based in Barcelona, Spain, tracking the foundation's grant from 2003 to 2020, reported that, the foundation has granted 6 billion USD, 5 billion of which was supposed to serve Africa. More worrisome, the CAS, which characterizes AFSA's interpretation of agroecology as "restrictive" and worse, has succeeded in undermining support for the paradigm among Africa's scientists and political leaders. Those of us at AFSA, in contrast, see our version of agroecology as liberating–based on farmers' rights to choose seeds and methods of cultivation, and free of corporate interference and control.

Through its Global Leadership Fellows Program, the CAS has trained 112 fellows to date, nearly two thirds recruited from Africa and many of them from countries where the biotech industry has been seeking regulatory approvals for GMOs: Nigeria, Uganda, Kenya and Ghana. In these critical battleground countries, CAS graduates work in media and government to argue that African governments should institute investment-friendly policies to help import the technologies that will rescue the continent's farmers from their anachronistic traditions.

Hunger in Africa derives from a single factor, CAS fellows argue: crop yields are relatively low. The reason is, first, that seeds bred and shared by farmers are unproductive, in their opinion; these should be replaced by GMOs. Second, African farmers do not use enough agrochemicals, a deficit that also needs remedy. And third, African farmers cultivate a multitude of crops to feed their families; if instead they focus on growing commodity crops for pan-African and global markets, they will get far better yields while addressing their nutrition and health concerns.

Fortified by linkages with another organization funded by the Gates Foundation, the Open Forum on Agriculture Biotechnology (OFAB), CAS fellows end up narrowing the democratic space for discussion of food systems in African countries. Opposing points of view are irrational, unscientific and harmful, they often insist. OFAB is an offshoot of the African Agricultural Technology Foundation, which was born in 2001 out of negotiations to promote GM seeds in Africa between the Rockefeller Foundation and corporations including Monsanto, Dupont, Pioneer and Syngenta. To our minds, these and other connections suggest that the Gates Foundation's resources help further the interests of multinational corporations interested in opening our markets for agrochemicals, synthetic fertilizers and genetically engineered seeds more than they assist farmers.

In Uganda, for example, the CAS has recruited journalists and key government individuals working on agriculture, science and technology to the cause of promoting GM seeds. Fellows write disparaging articles on agroecology, describing it as a "dead end," and promote biotechnology-based solutions in its stead. In Nigeria, Alliance fellows work closely with OFAB's Nigeria Chapter, the National Biotechnology Development Agency, the Nigerian Institute of Public Relations and the Nigerian Institute of Management to advocate for biotechnology, often characterizing it as the only scientific option.

The truth is, India's Green Revolution never was the runaway success it was advertised to be, as ongoing protests by the country's farmers underscore. And in Africa as well, the promises of prosperity through resource-intensive, commercialized agriculture have failed to materialize, according to data on the Alliance for the Green Revolution in Africa (AGRA) compiled by the Tufts Global Development and Environment Institute. AGRA was launched in 2006 by the Rockefeller Foundation and the Gates Foundation with the stated objective of increasing investment in Africa to reduce poverty and hunger. An analysis of the AGRA data by African and German civil society groups noted that, after 14 years of existence and over a billion dollars of investment, there is no evidence of an increase in income of small-scale producers and no significant enhancement of productivity in the countries that AGRA serves. Instead, the number of undernourished people increased by 31 percent, adverse environmental impacts appear to be considerable and crop diversity has declined.

These civil society groups called on donor and African governments to instead shift their support to programs that help small-scale food producers develop climate-resilient and ecologically sustainable farming practices. Similarly, a September 2020 report by the U.N. Food and Agriculture Organization recommends "promoting local food productions and short supply chains and a greater degree of self-sufficiency" in order to make food systems more resilient during the COVID-19 pandemic.

We welcome investment in agriculture on our continent, but we seek it in a form that is democratic and responsive to the people at the heart of agriculture, not as a top-down force that ends up concentrating power and profit into the hands of a small number of multinational companies. While describing how GM seeds and other technology would solve hunger in African countries, Bill Gates claimed that "it's a sovereign decision. No one makes that for them." But the massive resources of the Gates Foundation, which he co-chairs, have had an outsized influence on African scientists and policymakers, with the result that food systems on our continent are becoming ever more market-oriented and corporate-controlled.

This transformation has immense adverse implications for the nutrition, health, environment, culture and right to food of Africans. We ask that Gates let the continent's food producers and consumers chart our own paths toward sustainable and healthy farming practices and diets.

This is an opinion and analysis article; the views expressed by the author or authors are not necessarily those of Scientific American.

About the Authors

Million Belay, Ph.D., is the general coordinator of the Alliance for Food Sovereignty in Africa.

Bridget Mugambe is the Alliance for Food Sovereignty in Africa's program coordinator.

Section 4: Food Systems and the Environment

Can We Feed the World and Sustain the Planet?

By Jonathan A. Foley

Right now about one billion people suffer from chronic hunger. the world's farmers grow enough food to feed them, but it is not properly distributed and, even if it were, many cannot afford it, because prices are escalating.

But another challenge looms.

By 2050 the world's population will increase by two billion or three billion, which will likely double the demand for food, according to several studies. Demand will also rise because many more people will have higher incomes, which means they will eat more, especially meat. Increasing use of cropland for biofuels will put additional demands on our farms. So even if we solve today's problems of poverty and access—a daunting task—we will also have to produce twice as much to guarantee adequate supply worldwide.

And that's not all.

By clearing tropical forests, farming marginal lands, and intensifying industrial farming in sensitive landscapes and watersheds, humankind has made agriculture the planet's dominant environmental threat. Agriculture already consumes a large percentage of the earth's land surface and is destroying habitat, using up freshwater, polluting rivers and oceans, and emitting greenhouse gases more extensively than almost any other human activity. To guarantee the globe's long-term health, we must dramatically reduce agriculture's adverse impacts.

The world's food system faces three incredible, interwoven challenges. It must guarantee that all seven billion people alive today are adequately fed; it must double food production in the next 40 years; and it must achieve both goals while becoming truly environmentally sustainable.

Could these simultaneous goals possibly be met? An international team of experts, which I coordinated, has settled on five steps that, if pursued together, could raise by more than 100 percent the food available for human consumption globally, while significantly lessening greenhouse gas emissions, biodiversity losses, water use and water pollution. Tackling the triple challenge will be one of the most important tests humanity has ever faced. It is fair to say that our response will determine the fate of our civilization.

Bumping Up against Barriers

At first blush, the way to feed more people would seem clear: grow more food, by expanding farmland and improving yield—the amount of crops harvested per hectare. Unfortunately, the world is running into significant barriers on both counts.

Society already farms roughly 38 percent of the earth's land surface, not counting Greenland or Antarctica. Agriculture is by far the biggest human use of land on the planet; nothing else comes close. And most of that 38 percent covers the *best* farmland. Much of the remainder is covered by deserts, mountains, tundra, ice, cities, parks and other unsuitable growing areas. The few remaining frontiers are mainly in tropical forests and savannas, which are vital to the stability of the globe, especially as stores of carbon and biodiversity. Expanding into those areas is not a good idea, yet over the past 20 years five million to 10 million hectares of cropland a year have been created, with a significant portion of that amount in the tropics. These additions enlarged the net area of cultivated land by only 3 percent, however, because of farmland losses caused by urban development and other forces, particularly in temperate zones.

Improving yield also sounds enticing. Yet our research team found that average global crop yield increased by about 20 percent in the past 20 years—far less than what is typically reported. That improvement is significant, but the rate is nowhere near enough to double food production by midcentury. Whereas yields of some crops improved substantially, others saw little gain and a few even declined.

Feeding more people would be easier if all the food we grew went into human hands. But only 60 percent of the world's crops are meant for people: mostly grains, followed by pulses (beans, lentils), oil plants, vegetables and fruits. Another 35 percent is used for animal feed, and the final 5 percent goes to biofuels and other industrial products. Meat is the biggest issue here. Even with the most efficient meat and dairy systems, feeding crops to animals reduces the world's potential food supply. Typically grain-fed cattle operations use 30 kilograms of grain to make one kilogram of edible, boneless beef. Chicken and pork are more efficient, and grass-fed beef converts nonfood material into protein. No matter how you slice it, though, grain-fed meat production systems are a drain on the global food supply.

Another deterrent to growing more food is damage to the environment, which is already extensive. Only our use of energy, with its profound impacts on climate and ocean acidification, rivals the sheer magnitude of agriculture's environmental impacts. Our research team estimates that agriculture has already cleared or radically transformed 70 percent of the world's prehistoric grasslands, 50 percent of the savannas, 45 percent of the temperate deciduous forests and 25 percent of the tropical forests. Since the last ice age, nothing has disrupted ecosystems more. Agriculture's physical footprint is nearly 60 times that of the world's pavements and buildings.

Freshwater is another casualty. Humans use an astounding 4,000 cubic kilometers of water per year, mostly withdrawn from rivers and aquifers. Irrigation accounts for 70 percent of the draw. If we count only consumptive water use—water that is used and not returned to the watershed—irrigation climbs to 80 or 90 percent of the total. As a result, many large rivers, such as the Colorado, have diminished flows, some have dried up altogether, and many places have rapidly declining water tables, including regions of the U.S. and India.

Water is not only disappearing, it is being contaminated. Fertilizers, herbicides and pesticides are being spread at incredible levels and are found in nearly every ecosystem. The flows of nitrogen and phosphorus through the environment have more than doubled since 1960, causing widespread water pollution and enormous hypoxic "dead zones" at the mouths of many of the world's major rivers. Ironically, fertilizer runoff from farmland–in the name of growing more food–compromises another crucial source of nutrition: coastal fishing grounds. Fertilizer certainly has been a key ingredient of the green revolution that has helped feed the world, but when nearly half the fertilizer we apply runs off rather than nourishes crops, we clearly can do better.

Agriculture is also the largest single source of greenhouse gas emissions from society, collectively accounting for about 35 percent of the carbon dioxide, methane and nitrous oxide we release. That is more than the emissions from worldwide transportation (including all cars, trucks and planes) or electricity generation. The energy used to grow, process and transport food is a concern, but the vast majority of emissions comes from tropical deforestation, methane released from animals and rice paddies, and nitrous oxide from overfertilized soils.

Five Solutions

Modern agriculture has been an incredibly positive force in the world, but we can no longer ignore its dwindling ability to expand or the mounting environmental harm it imposes. Previous approaches to solving food and environmental issues were often at odds. We could boost food production by clearing more land or using more water and chemicals but only at a cost to the environment. Or we could restore ecosystems by taking farmland out of cultivation but only by reducing food production. This either-or approach is no longer acceptable. We need truly integrated solutions.

After many months of research and deliberation–based on analysis of newly generated global agricultural and environmental data–our international team has settled on a five-point plan for dealing with food and environmental challenges together.

Stop Expanding Agriculture's Footprint

Our first recommendation is to slow and ultimately stop the expansion of agriculture, particularly into tropical forests and savannas. The demise of these ecosystems has far-reaching impacts on the environment, especially through lost biodiversity and increased carbon dioxide emissions (from clearing land).

Slowing deforestation would dramatically reduce environmental damage while imposing only minor constraints on global food production. The resulting dip in farm capacity could be offset by reducing the displacement of more productive croplands by urbanization, degradation and abandonment.

Many proposals have been made to reduce deforestation. One of the most promising is the Reducing Emissions from Deforestation and Degradation (REDD) mechanism. Under REDD, rich nations pay tropical nations to protect their rain forests, in exchange for carbon credits. Other mechanisms include developing certification standards for agricultural products so that supply chains can be assured that crops were not grown on lands created by deforestation. Also, better biofuel policy that relies on nonfood crops such as switchgrass instead of food crops could make vital farmland newly available.

Close the World's Yield Gaps

To double global food production without expanding agriculture's footprint, we must significantly improve yields of existing farmlands. Two options exist: We can boost the productivity of our best farms–raising their "yield ceiling" through improved crop genetics and management. Or we can improve the yields of the world's least productive farms–closing the "yield gap" between a farm's current yield and its higher potential yield. The second option provides the largest and most immediate gain–especially in regions where hunger is most acute.

Our research team has analyzed global patterns of crop yields and found that much of the world has a significant yield gap. In particular, yields could increase substantially across many parts of

Africa, Central America and eastern Europe. In these regions, better seeds, more effective fertilizer application and efficient irrigation could produce much more food on the same amount of land. Our analysis suggests that closing the yield gap for the world's top 16 crops could increase total food production by 50 to 60 percent, with little environmental damage.

Reducing yield gaps in the least productive agricultural lands may often require some additional fertilizer and water. Care will have to be taken to avoid unbridled irrigation and chemical use. Many other techniques can improve yield. "Reduced tillage" planting techniques disturb less soil, preventing erosion. Cover crops planted between food-crop seasons reduce weeds and add nutrients and nitrogen to the soil when plowed under. Lessons from organic and agroecological systems can also be adopted, such as leaving crop residues on fields so that they decompose into nutrients. To close the world's yield gaps, we also have to overcome serious economic and social challenges, including better distribution of fertilizer and seed varieties to farms in impoverished regions and improving access to global markets for many regions.

Use Resources Much More Efficiently

To reduce the environmental impacts of agriculture, low- and high-yield regions alike must practice agriculture with vastly greater efficiency: far more crop output per unit of water, fertilizer and energy.

On average, it takes about one liter of irrigation water to grow one calorie of food, although some places use much more. Our analysis finds that farms can significantly curb water use without much reduction in food production, especially in dry climates. Primary strategies include drip irrigation (where water is applied directly to the plant's base and not wastefully sprayed into the air); mulching (covering the soil with organic matter to retain moisture); and reducing water lost from irrigation systems (by lessening evaporation from canals and reservoirs).

With fertilizers, we face a kind of Goldilocks problem. Some places have too few nutrients and therefore poor crop production, whereas others have too much, leading to pollution. Almost no one uses fertilizers "just right." Our analysis shows hotspots on the planet–particularly in China, northern India, the central U.S. and western Europe–where farmers could substantially reduce fertilizer use with little or no impact on food production. Amazingly, only 10 percent of the world's cropland generates 30 to 40 percent of agriculture's fertilizer pollution.

Among the actions that can fix this excess are policy and economic incentives, such as payments to farmers for watershed stewardship and protection, for reducing excessive fertilizer use, for improving manure management (especially manure storage, so that less runs off into the watershed during a storm), for capturing excess nutrients through recycling, and for instituting other conservation practices. In addition, restoring wetlands will enhance their capacity to act as a natural sponge to filter out nutrients in runoff.

Here again reduced tillage can help nourish the soil, as can precision agriculture (applying fertilizer and water only when and where they are needed and most effective) and organic farming techniques.

Shift Diets Away from Meat

We can dramatically increase global food availability and environmental sustainability by using more of our crops to feed people directly and less to fatten livestock.

Globally, humans could net up to three quadrillion additional calories every year–a 50 percent increase from our current supply–by switching to all-plant diets. Naturally, our current diets and uses of crops have many economic and social benefits, and our preferences are unlikely to change completely. Still, even small shifts in diet, say, from grain-fed beef to poultry, pork or pasture-fed beef, can pay off handsomely.

Reduce Food Waste

A final, obvious but often neglected recommendation is to reduce waste in the food system. Roughly 30 percent of the food produced on the planet is discarded, lost, spoiled or consumed by pests.

In rich countries, much of the waste takes place at the consumer end of the system, in restaurants and trash cans. Simple changes in our daily consumption patterns–reducing oversize portions, food thrown in the garbage, and the number of takeout and restaurant meals–could significantly trim losses, as well as our expanding waistlines. In poorer countries, the losses are similar in size but occur at the producer end, in the form of failed crops, stockpiles ruined by pests, or food that is never delivered because of bad infrastructure and markets. Improved storage, refrigeration and distribution systems can cut waste appreciably. Moreover, better market tools can connect people who have crops to those who need them, such as cell-phone systems in Africa that link suppliers, traders and purchasers.

Although completely eliminating waste from farm to fork is not realistic, even small steps would be extremely beneficial. Targeted efforts–especially reducing waste of the most resource-intensive foods such as meat and dairy–could make a big difference.

Moving toward a Networked Food System

In principle, our five-point strategy can address many food security and environmental challenges. Together the steps could increase the world's food availability by 100 to 180 percent, while significantly lowering greenhouse gas emissions, biodiversity losses, water use and water pollution.

It is important to emphasize that all five points (and perhaps more) must be pursued together. No single strategy is sufficient to solve all our problems. Think silver buckshot, not a silver bullet. We have tremendous successes from the green revolution and industrial-scale agriculture to build on, along with innovations in organic farming and local food systems. Let's take the best ideas and incorporate them into a new approach–a sustainable food system that focuses on nutritional, social and environmental performance, to bring responsible food production to scale.

We can configure this next-generation system as a network of local agricultural systems that are sensitive to nearby climate, water resources, ecosystems and culture and that are connected through efficient means of global trade and transport. Such a system could be resilient and also pay farmers a living wage.

One device that would help foster this new food system would be the equivalent of the Leadership in Energy and Environmental Design program now in place for constructing new commercial buildings sustainably. This LEED program awards increasingly higher levels of certification based on points that are accumulated by incorporating any of a wide range of green options, from solar power and efficient lighting to recycled building materials and low construction waste.

For sustainable agriculture, foods would be awarded points based on how well they deliver nutrition, food security and other public benefits, minus their environmental and social costs. This certification would help us get beyond current food labels such as "local" and "organic," which really do not tell us much about what we are eating. Instead we can look at the whole performance of our food–across nutritional, social and environmental dimensions–and weigh the costs and benefits of different farming approaches.

Imagine the possibilities: sustainable citrus and coffee from the tropics, connected to sustainable cereals from the temperate zone, supplemented by locally grown greens and root vegetables, all grown under transparent, performance-based standards. Use your smartphone and the latest sustainable food app, and you will learn where your food came from, who grew it, how it was grown, and how it ranks against various social, nutritional and environmental criteria. And when you find food that works, you can tweet about it to your social network of farmers and foodies.

The principles and practices of our different agricultural systems–from large-scale commercial to local and organic–provide the foundation for grappling with the world's food security and environmental needs. Feeding nine billion people in a truly sustainable way will be one of the greatest challenges our civilization has had to confront. It will require the imagination, determination and hard work of countless people from all over the world. There is no time to lose.

About the Author

Jonathan A. Foley is director of the Institute on the Environment at the University of Minnesota, where he is also McKnight Presidential Chair of Global Sustainability.

Here's How Much Food Contributes to Climate Change

By Andrea Thompson

As with most things related to people, the food we eat comes with a carbon cost. Soil tillage, crop and livestock transportation, manure management and all the other aspects of global food production generate greenhouse gas emissions to the tune of more than 17 billion metric tons per year, according to a new study published on Monday in *Nature Food*. Animal-based foods account for 57 percent of those emissions, and plant-based ones make up 29 percent. The researchers hope the paper's detailed breakdown of how much each agricultural practice, animal product, crop and country contributes to carbon emissions can help focus and fine-tune reduction efforts.

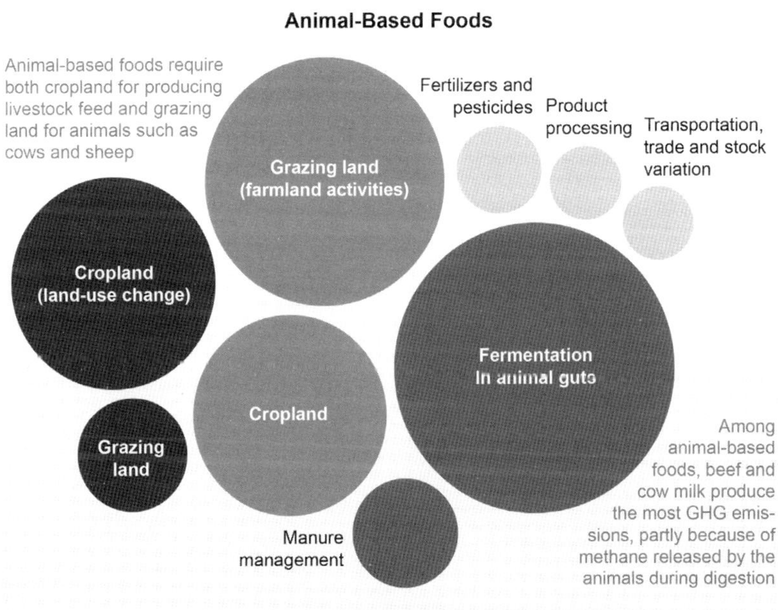

Credit: Amanda Montañez; Source: "Global Greenhouse Gas Emissions from Animal-Based Foods Are Twice Those of Plant-Based Foods," by Xiaoming Xu et al., in Nature Food. Published online September 13, 2021

Though previous studies have estimated emissions from agriculture, the authors say this work is more detailed and comprehensive. It uses data on 171 crops and 16 animal products from more than 200 countries, along with computer modeling, to calculate the amounts of carbon dioxide, methane and nitrous oxide that are contributed by individual elements of the global food system, including consumption and production. If we want to control those emissions, "we needed to calculate a good baseline," says study co-author Atul Jain, a climate scientist at the University of Illinois at Urbana-Champaign.

The results align with other research, says Liqing Peng, a food and agriculture modeler at the nonprofit World Resources Institute, which published its own report on agricultural emissions in 2019. The new study's estimate of total emissions is on the higher side of the range of previous ones, she says. This is partly because it includes data on farmland management practices, such as irrigation and planting, as well as activities beyond the farm, such as processing and packaging–numbers which are difficult to obtain. "It's really important to get as detailed as possible on these breakdowns" in order to know where to concentrate emissions-reduction research and policies, Peng adds.

Of the food products the study examined, beef production was the top emissions contributor by a wide margin, accounting for 25 percent of the total. Among animal-based products, it was followed by cow milk, pork and chicken meat, in that order. In the category of crops, rice farming was the top contributor–and it was the second-highest contributor among all products, accounting for 12 percent of the total. Rice's relatively high ranking comes from the methane-producing bacteria that thrive in the anaerobic conditions of flooded paddies. After rice, the highest emissions associated with plant production came from wheat, sugarcane and maize.

As for contributions from individual regions, South and Southeast Asia comprised the overall top emitter of greenhouse gases related to food production and the only region where plant-based emissions were higher than animal-based ones because of rice cultivation. Among

The Emissions Footprint of Food

Every aspect of the production and consumption of food has an impact carbon emissions. Here, the emissions from both plant-based and animal-based food are broken down by the various practices that are involved in the global food system, from tilling soil to producing fertilizer to transporting products.

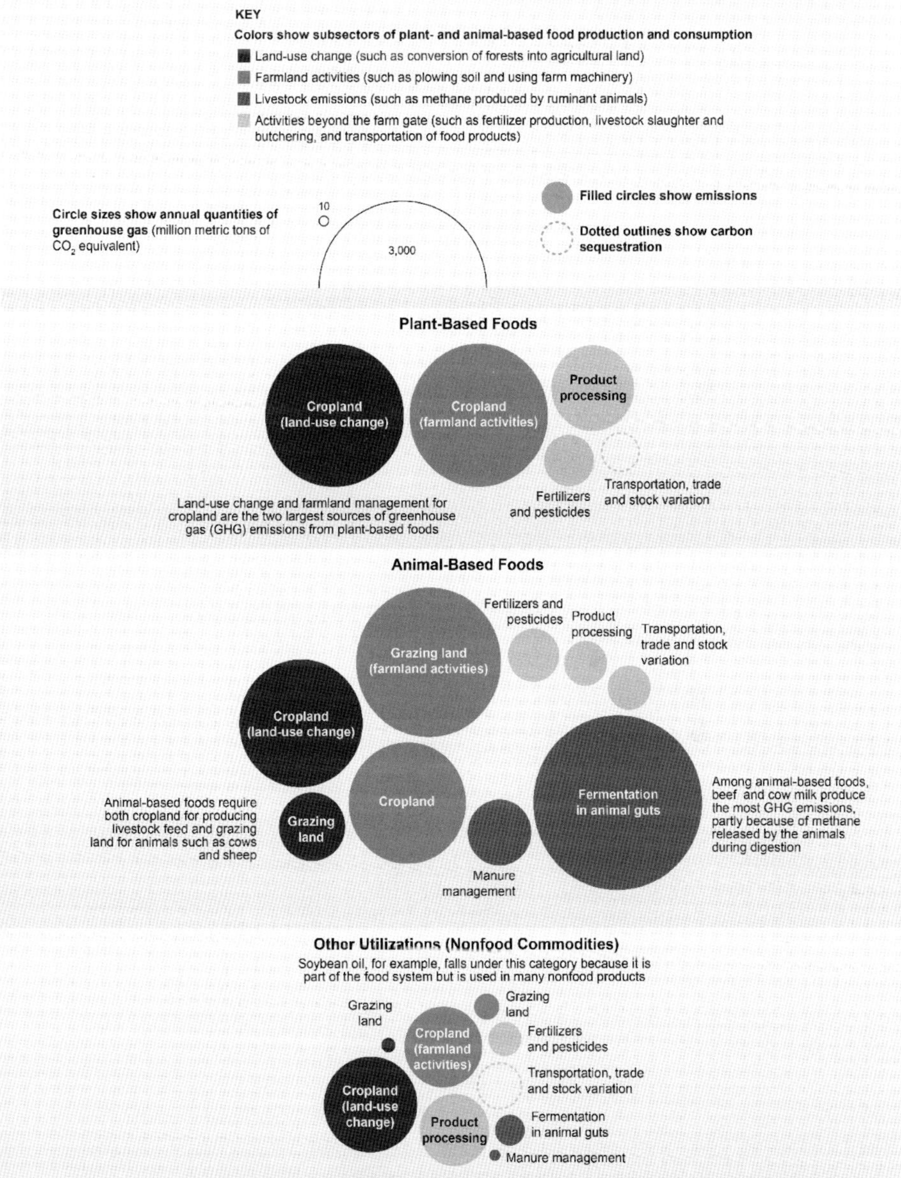

Credit: Amanda Montañez; Source: "Global Greenhouse Gas Emissions from Animal-Based Foods Are Twice Those of Plant-Based Foods," by Xiaoming Xu et al., in Nature Food. Published online September 13, 2021

countries, China, India and Indonesia had the highest plant-based food production emissions. This, again, was linked to rice farming, as well as large populations that create a high demand for food–which drives more conversion of land to agricultural production. Because of their large populations, these areas registered relatively low per capita production emissions. The highest per capita emissions (and the second-highest regional emissions overall) were found in South America because of its relatively large production of meat, particularly beef. North America had the second-highest per capita production emissions, followed by Europe.

The study also broke down emissions caused by various aspects of food production and consumption. Farm activities, such as plowing soil or using other types of equipment–along with the conversion of land from forests or other natural landscapes into pasture and cropland–collectively accounted for two thirds of emissions.

Jain and his colleagues want to use these results, along with computer modeling, to examine how changing farmland management (reducing fertilizer use or employing no-till soil methods, for example) could reduce emissions. They also want to study how to balance the food requirements of a growing global population with the need to halt deforestation. "That's why we put so much effort" into being so comprehensive in the new paper's accounting, Jain says. His co-author Xiaoming Xu, also at the University of Illinois at Urbana-Champaign, is optimistic about the prospects of making a dent in food-based emissions. "I think there are a lot of options we can do," he says. But Peng notes that meeting the current–and ambitious–international emissions-reduction targets will mean figuring out which approaches not only make the most economic sense but also provide the biggest bang for the buck in terms of getting results. "You want to do everything," she says, "but you can't do everything at the same time."

About the Author

Andrea Thompson, an associate editor at Scientific American, *covers sustainability.*

These Plants Can Replace Meat—but Will Doing So Help the Environment?

By Shannon Hall

It pays to be a picky eater–at least, when it comes to meat. A study published Thursday in *Scientific Reports* suggests that certain plant-based diets can provide the same amount of nutrition as meat products and simultaneously protect the environment. While experts agree that meatless meals provide myriad benefits, going vegetarian is not a realistic option for many. Nor will it do much to slow down climate change.

There is no question that the growth of livestock farming and meat consumption is far from environmentally friendly. For one thing, forests are often cut down to make way for pastures, reducing biodiversity and natural carbon sinks. Also, livestock are typically fed corn, soybean meal and other grains–which first have to be grown using fertilizers, fuels, pesticides, water and land. Even their manure emits a hefty percentage of greenhouse gases. All in all, a recent study suggested that livestock produce as much as 80 percent of all food-related emissions.

But despite this mounting evidence, many are hesitant to take the meat-free leap. Gidon Eshel, a research professor of environmental and urban studies at Bard College, contends this attitude is largely because people question whether their meals would still be nutritionally sound. So he and his colleagues took a deeper look at the issue by determining the precise plant-based diet that would allow someone to swallow every nutrient (including proteins, vitamins and fatty acids) they would in a carnivorous one. They then calculated the environmental impacts if all Americans were to hypothetically make such a shift. "It's really the next frontier in this business–to simultaneously address the nutritional and environmental issues at the same time," Eshel says.

To start, his team built a computer algorithm that sorted through 73 different plant- and animal-based foods to pinpoint a vegetarian diet that could (nutritionally speaking) replace either beef alone or beef, poultry and pork. Doing so was not as hard as it might seem; Eshel and his colleagues found that a diet consisting predominantly of soy, green pepper, squash, buckwheat and asparagus could provide all the nutritional benefits of one that would often include a juicy steak. "You don't have to eat some bizarre concoction," Eshel says. "These are just naturally occurring plant-based foods."

Such a regimen could even boost human life spans, says Marco Springmann, a senior researcher on environmental sustainability and public health at the University of Oxford. Meat-based diets, he says, are associated with an increase in the incidence of type 2 diabetes, coronary heart disease and obesity, whereas legumes are associated with a decrease in the likelihood of developing many of these health outcomes.

The new study jibes with an Intergovernmental Panel on Climate Change (IPCC) report, also released on Thursday, that focuses on global warming impacts on the land, and vice versa. The authors of that report, too, highlighted the numerous environmental and health benefits of a plant-based diet. "You save on future climate-change damages," says Springmann, who was not involved with Eshel's recent study or the IPCC report. "You save on biodiversity impacts of deforestation. You save on chronic disease rates and therefore on your medical bills."

Eshel and his colleagues specifically found that if all Americans switched away from meat, it would eliminate the need for pastureland and reduce the amount of high-quality cropland under cultivation by as much as 25 percent–an area as large as Montana. But what truly excites Eshel is how dramatically the swap could clean the nation's waterways. Today excess nitrogen from fertilizer spills into rivers. This pollution causes toxic algal blooms that deplete oxygen, leaving vast dead zones that inflict tens of billions of dollars of economic damage. But many of the plants within Eshel's diet require far less nitrogen fertilizer than plants grown to feed livestock. Overall, the study says, a vegetarian shift could prevent roughly 4.5 billion kilograms of nitrogen from being discharged into U.S. waterways—a number far greater than the nitrogen currently rushing through the Mississippi en route to the Gulf of Mexico.

But Marty Matlock, a professor of ecological engineering at the University of Arkansas, who was not involved in the study, points out that Eshel and his colleagues' assessment does not reflect the reality of the U.S. food system. "This doesn't consider the impact of this sort of diet on those who can't afford to buy the vegetables," he says. "Just ask, 'Why do we have an obesity problem at the same time we have a food security problem?' Because the cheapest food you can eat is a McDonald's Happy Meal." There are many "food deserts," he says, where vegetables are expensive and even hard to find—not to mention the fact that it also takes an environmental toll to grow asparagus in Mexico or Peru before shipping it to the U.S. (Eshel's study did not consider this factor.) Instead Matlock argues that the best diet moving forward just might involve algae, which are not only packed with twice as much protein as meat, plus vitamins and minerals, but can be grown in nonpotable water. Matlock notes that we have even been eating algae—particularly seaweed—for thousands of years and that the recent proliferation of algal powders as food supplements suggests many people might be willing to jump onboard.

The authors of the new study do acknowledge that one of the environmental downsides to their proposed shift away from meat is that food-related water use would actually increase 15 percent. Moreover, although the change would reduce greenhouse gas emissions, it would only do so by 6 percent. "It won't buy you a get-out-of-jail solution to climate change," Eshel says. Matlock agrees, pointing out that the greenhouse gas contribution of the food system is a drop in the bucket as compared with burning fossil fuels. The focus, he says, should be on reducing that fossil-fuel use, updating our transportation grids and sequestering carbon in soil. “We need to keep our eye on that ball,” he adds, “and not get distracted by asparagus and green peppers.”

About the Author

Shannon Hall is an award-winning freelance science journalist based in the Rocky Mountains. She specializes in writing about astronomy, geology and the environment.

The Blue Food Revolution: Making Aquaculture a Sustainable Food Source

By Sarah Simpson

Neil Sims tends his rowdy stock like any devoted farmer. But rather than saddling a horse like the Australian sheep drovers he grew up with, Sims dons a snorkel and mask to wrangle his herd: 480,000 silver fish corralled half a mile off the Kona coast of Hawaii's Big Island.

Tucked discretely below the waves, Sims's farm is one of 20 operations worldwide that are trying to take advantage of the earth's last great agricultural frontier: the ocean. Their offshore locations offer a distinct advantage over the thousands of conventional fish farms—flotillas of pens that hug the coastline. Too often old-style coastal farms, scorned as eyesores and ocean polluters, exude enough fish excrement and food scraps to cloud the calm, shallow waters, triggering harmful algal blooms or snuffing out sea life underneath the pens. At offshore sites such as Kona Blue Water Farms, pollution is not an issue, Sims explains. The seven submerged paddocks, each one as big as a high school gymnasium, are anchored within rapid currents that sweep away the waste, which is quickly diluted to harmless levels in the open waters.

Rather than taking Sims's word for it, I put swim fins on my feet and a snorkel around my neck, high-step to the edge of his small service boat, and take the plunge. From the water, the double-cone-shape cage is aglow like a colossal Chinese lantern, with shimmering streams of sunlight and glinting forms of darting fish. To the touch, the material that stretches taut around the outside of the cage's frame feels more like a fence than a net. The solid, Kevlar-esque material would repel hungry sharks as effectively as it contains teeming masses of *Seriola rivoliana*, a local species of yellowtail that Kona Blue has domesticated as an alternative to wild tuna.

Why yellowtail? Many wild tuna fisheries are collapsing, and sushi-grade yellowtail fetches a high price. Sims and fellow marine biologist Dale Sarver founded Kona Blue in 2001 to raise popular fish sustainably. But the company's methods could just as well be applied to run-of-the-mill fish—and we may need them. The global population of 6.9 billion people is estimated to rise to 9.3 billion by 2050, and people with higher living standards also tend to eat more meat and seafood. Yet the global catch from wild fisheries has been stagnant or declining for a decade. Raising cows, pigs, chickens and other animals consumes vast amounts of land, freshwater, fossil fuels that pollute the air and fertilizers that run off and choke rivers and oceans.

Where will all the needed protein for people come from? The answer could well be new offshore farms, if they can function efficiently, and coastal farms, if they can be cleaned up.

Cleaner Is Better

To some scientists, feeding the world calls for transferring the production of our animal protein to the seas. If a blue food revolution is to fill such an exalted plate at the dinner table, however, it must operate in environmentally sound ways—and make its benefits better known both to a jaded public and to policy makers with the power to help or retard its spread.

In the past, condemnation might have been apt. When modern coastal fish farming began about 30 years ago, virtually no one was doing things right, either for the environment or for the industry's long-term sustainability. Fish sewage was just one of the issues. Shrimp farmers in Southeast Asia and Mexico clear-cut coastal mangrove forests to make ponds to grow their shrimp. In the salmon farms of Europe and the Americas, animals were often too densely packed, helping disease and parasites sweep through the populations. Fish that escaped farms sometimes spread their diseases to native species. Making matters worse, the aquaculture industry represented (and still does) a net drain on fish mass; wild forage fish—small, cheap species that humans do not prefer but that bigger, wild fish eat–are captured in large quantities and ground into feed for the bigger, tastier, more expensive farmed fish folks favor.

Clearly, such ills were not good for business, and the industry has devised innovative solutions. Kona Blue's strategy of situating the farm within rapid offshore currents is one example. Other farmers are beginning to raise seaweed and filter-feeding animals such as mollusks near the fish pens to gobble up waste. Throughout the industry, including freshwater pens, improvements in animal husbandry and feed formulations are reducing disease and helping fish grow faster, with less forage fish in their diets. It may still be a long time before environmental groups remove farmed fish from "don't buy" lists, however.

Some cutting-edge thinkers are experimenting with an even bolder move. Nations exercise sole rights to manage waters out to 200 nautical miles from their shores–a vast frontier untapped for domesticated food production. Around the U.S., that frontier measures 3.4 million square nautical miles. Submerged fish pens, steered by large propellers, could ride in stable ocean currents, returning months later to their starting points or a distant destination to deliver fresh fish for market.

Ocean engineer Clifford Goudey tested the world's first self-propelled, submersible fish pen off the coast of Puerto Rico in late 2008. A geodesic sphere 62 feet in diameter, the cage proved surprisingly maneuverable when outfitted with a pair of eight-foot propellers, says Goudey, former director of M.I.T. Sea Grant's Offshore Aquaculture Engineering Center. Goudey imagines launching dozens of mobile farms in a steady progression within a predictable current that traverses the Caribbean Sea every nine months.

Feeding Frenzy

The aspect of marine (saltwater) aquaculture that has been hardest to fix is the need to use small, wild fish as food for the large, farmed varieties. (The small fish are not farmed, because a mature industry already exists that catches and grinds them into fish meal and oil.) The feed issue comes into pungent focus for me when Sims and I climb aboard an old U.S. Navy transport ship cleverly transformed into a feeding barge. The sea swell pitches me sideways as I make my way to the bow, calling to mind a bumpy pickup truck ride I took long ago, across a semifrozen Missouri pasture to deliver hay to my cousin's Herefords. The memory of sweet-smelling dried grass vanishes when I grab a handful of oily brown feed from a 2,000-pound sack propped open on the deck. The pellets look like kibble for a small terrier but reek of an empty anchovy tin.

The odor is no surprise; 30 percent of Kona Blue's feed is ground up Peruvian anchovy. Yellowtail could survive on a vegetarian diet, but they wouldn't taste as good, Sims explains. Nor would their flesh include all the fatty acids and amino acids that make them healthy to eat. Those ingredients come from fish meal and fish oil, and that is the issue. "We are often pilloried because we're killing fish to grow fish," Sims says. Salmon farming, done in coastal pens, draws the same ire.

Detractors worry that rising demand from fish farms will wipe out wild anchovies, sardines and other forage fish. Before modern fish farming began, most fish meal was fed to pigs and chickens, but today aquaculture consumes 68 percent of the fish meal. Consumption has lessened under advanced feed formulas, however. When Kona Blue started raising yellowtail in 2005, its feed pellets were 80 percent anchovy. By early 2008 the company had reduced the share to 30 percent–without sacrificing taste or health benefit, Sims says–by increasing the concentration of soybean meal and adding chicken oil, a by-product of poultry processing. The compound feed pellets are a big improvement over the egregious practice of dumping whole sardines into the fish cages. Unfortunately, this wasteful habit remains the norm among less responsible farmers.

A goal for the more enlightened proprietors is a break-even ratio, in which the amount of fish in feed equals the weight of fish produced for market. Farmers of freshwater tilapia and catfish have attained this magic ratio, but marine farmers have not. Because

70 percent of Kona Blue's feed is agricultural protein and oil, it now needs only 1.6 to 2.0 pounds of anchovies to produce one pound of yellowtail. The average for the farmed salmon industry is around 3.0. To achieve no net loss of marine protein, the industry would have to reduce that ratio. Still, farmed fish take a far smaller bite than their wild equivalents do: over its lifetime, a wild tuna may consume as much as 100 pounds of food per pound of its own weight, all of it fish.

The pressure to reduce sardine and anchovy catches will increase as the number of fish farms grows. Aquaculture is the fastest-growing food production sector in the world, expanding at 7.5 percent a year since 1994. At that pace, fish meal and fish oil resources could be exhausted by 2040. An overarching goal, therefore, is to eliminate wild fish products from feed altogether, within a decade or so, asserts marine ecologist Carlos M. Duarte, who directs the International Laboratory for Global Change at the Spanish Council for Scientific Research in Majorca.

One breakthrough that could help is coaxing the coveted omega-3 fatty acid DHA out of microscopic algae, which could replace some of the forage fish content in feed. Advanced Bio-Nutrition in Columbia, Md., is testing feed that contains the same algae-derived DHA that enhances infant formula, milk and juice now sold in stores. Recently researchers at Australia's Commonwealth Scientific and Industrial Research Organization coaxed DHA out of land plants for the first time. Duarte suggests that fierce competition for agricultural land and freshwater means that fish farmers should eventually eliminate soy, chicken oil and other terrestrial products as well, instead feeding their flocks on zooplankton and seaweed, which is easy to grow. (Seaweed already accounts for nearly one quarter of all marine aquaculture value.)

Despite improvements in marine fish farming, prominent environmentalists and academics still shoot it down. Marine ecologist Jeremy Jackson of the Scripps Institution of Oceanography says he is "violently opposed" to aquaculture of predatory fish and shrimp—basically, any fish people like to eat sashimi-style. He calls the practice "environmentally catastrophic" in the pressure it puts on wild fish supplies and insists it should be "illegal."

Smarter Than Beef

Jackson's point, echoed by other critics, is that the risk of collapsing forage fisheries, which are already overexploited, is too great to justify serving up a luxury food most of the world will never taste. Far better would be to eat the herbivorous sardines and anchovies directly instead of farmed, top-end predators.

Sims agrees that we should *fish* lower on the food web but says that does not mean we need to *eat* lower. "Let's get real. I eat anchovies on my pizza, but I can't get anyone else in my family to do it," he says. "If you can get a pound of farmed sushi for every pound of anchovy, why not give people the thing they want to eat?"

Certain people scoff at fish consumption–whether wild-caught or farm-raised–on the premise that the planet and its human inhabitants would be healthier if people ate more plants. But society is not rushing to become vegetarian. More people are eating more meat, particularly as populations in the developing world become wealthier, more urban and more Western. The World Health Organization predicts a 25 percent increase in per capita meat consumption by 2050. Even if consumption held steady, crop and grazing areas would have to increase by 50 to 70 percent, at current yields, to produce the food required in 2050.

That reality begs for a comparison rarely made: fish farming versus terrestrial farming. Done right, fish farming could provide much needed protein for the world while minimizing the expansion of land-based farming and the attendant environmental costs.

Land-based farmers have already transformed 40 percent of the earth's terrestrial surface. And after 10,000 years to work out the kinks, major problems still abound. Cattle eat tremendous amounts of heavily fertilized crops, and pig and chicken farms are notorious polluters. The dead zones underneath coastal fish farms pale in comparison to the huge dead zones that fertilizer run-off triggers in the Gulf of Mexico, Black Sea and elsewhere and to the harmful algal blooms that pig farm effluent has caused in Chesapeake Bay.

A growing number of scientists are beginning to compare the environmental impacts of all the various protein production systems, so that society can "focus its energies on efficiently solving the most demanding problems," writes Kenneth M. Brooks, an independent aquatic environmental consultant in Port Townsend, Wash. Brooks estimates that raising Angus beef requires 4,400 times more high-quality pasture land than sea¬floor needed for the equivalent weight of farmed Atlantic salmon filets. What is more, the ecosystem below a salmon farm can recover in less than a decade, instead of the centuries it would take for a cattle pasture to revert to mature forest.

An even more compelling reason to raise protein in the sea may be to reduce humanity's drain on freshwater. As Duarte points out, animal meat products represent only 3.5 percent of food production but consume 45 percent of the water used in agriculture. By shifting most protein production to the ocean, he says, "land agriculture could grow considerably without exceeding current levels of water use."

Of course, collecting and transporting soybean meal and chicken oil and feeding fish flocks all consume energy and create emissions, too. Fuel consumption and emissions are greater for farms that are farther from shore, but both types of farming rate better than most fishing fleets. The only way offshore farmers can be profitable right now is to raise high-priced fish, but costs can come down: a few experimental farms are already raising cost-competitive mussels in the ocean.

Environmental Distinctions

If providing more fish to consumers is an answer to meeting global demands for protein, why not just catch more fish directly? Many wild fisheries are maxed out, right at a time when global population, as well as per capita demand for fish, is booming. North Americans, for example, are heeding health experts' advice to eat fish to help reduce the risk of heart attacks and improve brain function.

What is more, fishing fleets consume vast amounts of fuel and emit volumes of greenhouse gases and pollutants. Widely used, indiscriminate fishing methods, such as trawling and dredging, kill millions of animals; studies indicate that at least half the sea life fishers haul in this way is discarded as too small, overquota or the wrong species. All too often this so-called by-catch is dead by the time it is tossed overboard. Aquaculture eliminates this waste altogether: "Farmers only harvest the fish in their pens," Sims notes.

Goudey points out another often overlooked reality: you can grow fish more efficiently than you can catch them. Farmed fish convert food into flesh much more effectively than their wild brethren, which expend enormous amounts of energy as they hunt for food and evade predators, seek a mate and reproduce. Farmed fish have it easy by comparison, so most of their diet goes into growth.

Kona Blue's yellowtail and most farmed salmon are between one and three years old at harvest, one-third the age of the large, wild tuna targeted for sushi. The younger age also means farmed fish have less opportunity to accumulate mercury and other persistent pollutants that can make mature tuna and swordfish a potential health threat.

Indeed, fish farming already accounts for 47 percent of the seafood people consume worldwide, up from only 9 percent in 1980. Experts predict the share could rise to 62 percent of the total protein supply by 2050. "Clearly, aquaculture is big, and it is here to stay. People who are against it really aren't getting it," says Jose Villalon, aquaculture director at the World Wildlife Fund. Looking only at the ills of aquaculture is misleading if they are not compared with the ills of other forms of food production. Aquaculture affects the earth, and no number of improvements will eliminate all problems. But every food production system taxes the environment, and wild fish, beef, pork and poultry producers impose some of the greatest burdens.

To encourage good practices and help distinguish clean fish farms from the worst offenders, the World Wildlife Fund has co-founded the Aquaculture Stewardship Council to set global standards for responsible practices and to use independent auditors to certify compliant farms. The council's first set of standards is expected early this year. The council believes certification could have the greatest effect by motivating the world's 100 to 200 big seafood retailers to buy fish from certified farms, rather than trying to crack down directly on thousands of producers.

The Ocean Conservancy's aquaculture director George Leonard agrees that this kind of farm-to-plate certification program is an important way to encourage fish farmers to pursue better sustainability practices. As in any global industry, he says, cheap, unscrupulous providers will always exist. Setting a regulatory "floor" could require U.S. farmers to behave responsibly "without making it impossible for them to compete."

That point is key. Only five of the world's 20 offshore installations are in U.S. waters. Goudey thinks more aquaculture entrepreneurs would dive in if the U.S. put a licensing system into place for federal waters, from three nautical miles offshore to the 200-mile boundary. "No investor is going to back a U.S. operation when there are no statutes granting rights of tenancy to an operation," Goudey asserts. All U.S. farms exist inside the three-mile-wide strip of water that states control, and only a few states, such as Hawaii, allow them. California has yet to grant permits, despite government estimates that a sustainable offshore fish-farming industry in less than 1 percent of the state's waters could bring in up to $1 billion a year.

Protein Policy

To grow, and do so sustainably, the fish-farming industry will need appropriate policies and a fairer playing field. At the moment, robust government fuel subsidies keep trawling and dredging fleets alive, despite their well-known destruction of the seafloor and the terrible volume of dead by-catch. Farm subsidies help to keep beef, pork and poultry production profitable. And powerful farm lobbies continue to block attempts to curtail the flow of nitrogen-rich fertilizer down the Mississippi River. "Almost none of these more traditional ways of producing food have received the scrutiny that aquaculture has," Brooks says. The public has accepted domestication of the land but maintains that the ocean is a wild frontier to be left alone, even though this imbalance may not be the most sustainable plan for feeding the world.

Policy shifts at the federal and regional levels may soon open up U.S. federal waters. In January 2009 the Gulf of Mexico Fishery Management Council voted in favor of an unprecedented plan for permitting offshore aquaculture within its jurisdiction, pending approval from higher levels within the U.S. National Oceanic and Atmospheric Administration. NOAA will evaluate the plan only after it finalizes its new national aquaculture policy, which addresses all forms of the industry and will probably include guidance for the development of a consistent, nationwide framework for regulating commercial activities. "We don't want the blue revolution to repeat the mistakes of the green revolution," says NOAA director Jane Lubchenco. "It's too important to get it wrong, and there are so many ways to get it wrong."

Given relentlessly rising demand, society has to make hard choices about where greater protein production should occur. "One of my goals has been to get us to a position where, when people say food security, they don't just mean grains and livestock but also fisheries and aquaculture," Lubchenco says. Duarte suggests we take some pressure off the land and turn to the seas, where we have the opportunity to do aquaculture right, rather than looking back 40 years from now wishing we had done so.

As for Neil Sims's part of the blue food revolution, he is courting technology companies for upgrades. Tools such as robotic net cleaners, automated feeders and satellite-controlled video cameras to monitor fish health and cage damage would help Kona Blue's crew manage its offshore farms remotely. "Not just so we can grow more fish in the ocean," Sims says. "So we can grow more fish *better*."

About the Author

Sarah Simpson is a freelance writer and contributing editor for Scientific American. *She lives in Riverside, Calif.*

GLOSSARY

aquaculture The cultivation of living things naturally occurring in water.

chronic Continuing or occurring again and again for a long time.

dredging Pulling things up from the bottom of the ocean.

effluent Liquid discharged as waste.

ethanol A colorless, flammable, easily evaporated liquid that has a variety of uses, including in fuel.

finite In limited supply.

hubris Exaggerated, undeserved pride.

inefficient Wasteful of time or energy.

organic Relating to, producing, dealing in, or involving foods produced with the use of feed or fertilizer obtained from plants or animals and without the use of laboratory-made fertilizers, growth substances, antibiotics, or pesticides.

paltry An amount small enough to be worthless.

perennial In plants, living for several years, usually with new leafy growth produced from the base each year.

sequester To bind or absorb carbon dioxide as part of a larger chemical process or compound.

serum Blood plasma from which certain substances involved in the clotting of blood have been removed.

teeming Filled with.

FURTHER INFORMATION

"Food Systems," OECD, www.oecd.org/food-systems.

"Future Food Systems: For People, Our Planet, and Prosperity," Global Panel on Agriculture and Food Systems for Nutrition, foresight.glopan.org.

"Science and History of GMOs and Other Food Modification Processes," FDA, April 19, 2023, www.fda.gov/food/agricultural-biotechnology/science-and-history-gmos-and-other-food-modification-processes.

"What Is the Food System?," Oxford Martin Programme on the Future of Food, www.futureoffood.ox.ac.uk/what-food-system.

"What You Need to Know about Food Security and Climate Change," World Bank, October 17, 2022, www.worldbank.org/en/news/feature/2022/10/17/what-you-need-to-know-about-food-security-and-climate-change.

Chandrasekhar, Aruna, Daisy Dunne, and Giuliana Viglione. "UN Land Report: Five Key Takeaways for Climate Change, Food Systems and Nature Loss," CarbonBrief, April 27, 2022, www.carbonbrief.org/un-land-report-five-key-takeaways-for-climate-change-food-systems-and-nature-loss.

Ranney, Marcus, and Sahil Shah. "The Future of Food: Imagining Our Food System in the Decades to Come," Atlantic Council, December 20, 2022, www.atlanticcouncil.org/blogs/geotech-cues/imagining-our-food-system-in-the-decades-to-come.

Wadwha, Vivek, and Alex Salkever. "The Gene-Editing Technology in Your Store-Bought Tomatoes That Could Eat Agriculture," *Fortune*, February 7, 2023, fortune.com/2023/02/27/the-gene-editing-technology-in-your-store-bought-tomatoes-that-could-eat-agriculture.

CITATIONS

1.1 Our Food Systems Are in Crisis by Izabella Koziell (October 15, 2019); 1.2 The Effects of COVID-19 Will Ripple through Food Systems by Laura Poppick (March 26, 2020); 1.3 How to Make the Food System More Energy Efficient by Michael E. Webber (January 1, 2012); 1.4 Feeding a Hot, Hungry Planet by Lisa Palmer (May 22, 2017); 1.5 Long Live Microbiomes! by Louise Maher-Johnson and Ayana Elizabeth Johnson (September 3, 2019); 2.1 Growing Skyscrapers: The Rise of Vertical Farms by Dickson Despommier (November 1, 2009); 2.2 The Future of Farming by Andrew Sharpley (November 22, 2019); 2.3 Agroecology Is the Solution to World Hunger by Raj Patel (September 22, 2021); 2.4 Test-Tube Burger: Lab-Cultured Meat Passes Taste Test (Sort of) by Arielle Duhaime-Ross (August 5, 2013); 2.5 Tweaking Vegetables' Genes Could Make Them Tastier—And You'll Get to Try Them Soon by Meghan Bartels (May 10, 2023); 2.6 Faux Fish Might Help Aquaculture Keep Feeding the World by Leslie Nemo (March 6, 2019); 2.7 Spray-On, Rinse-Off Food 'Wrapper' Can Cut Plastic Packaging by Sam Jones (June 24, 2022); 2.8 Advanced Food Tracking and Packaging Will Save Lives and Cut Waste by Rona Chandrawati and Bernard S. Meyerson (July 1, 2019); 3.1 Organically Speaking: The Marketing Language of Organic Food by Layla Eplett (August 1, 2016); 3.2 Does the World Need GM Foods? by Sasha Nemecek (December 1, 2006); 3.3 The Truth about Genetically Modified Food by David H. Freedman (September 1, 2013); 3.4 Do Seed Companies Control GM Crop Research? by The Editors (August 1, 2009); 3.5 How Biotech Crops Can Crash—and Still Never Fail by Aniket Aga and Maywa Montenegro de Wit (December 27, 2021); 3.6 Designer Crops of the Future Must Be Better Tailored for Women in Agriculture by Vivian Polar and Matty Demont (July 25, 2022); 3.7 Should the Concept of a Food Desert Be Deserted? by Layla Eplett (August 1, 2016); 3.8 Bill Gates Should Stop Telling Africans What Kind of Agriculture Africans Need by Million Belay and Bridget Mugambe (July 6, 2021); 4.1 Can We Feed the World and Sustain the Planet? by Jonathan A. Foley (November 1, 2011); 4.2 Here's How Much Food Contributes to Climate Change by Andrea Thompson (September 13, 2021); 4.3 These Plants Can Replace Meat—but Will Doing So Help the Environment? by Shannon Hall (August 8, 2019); 4.4 The Blue Food Revolution: Making Aquaculture a Sustainable Food Source by Sarah Simpson (February 1, 2011).

Each author biography was accurate at the time the article was originally published.

INDEX

E

F

G

H

I

T

U

V

W